WRESTLING WITH
GRACE

D0110387

WRESTLING WITH
GRACE

A Spirituality for
the Rough Edges
of Daily Life

ROBERT CORIN MORRIS

UPPER
ROOM BOOKS®
NASHVILLE

Cover and interior design: Gore Studio, Inc., Nashville
First printing: 2003

Library of Congress Cataloging-in-Publication Data
Morris, Robert Corin, 1941–
    Wrestling with grace : a spirituality for the rough edges of daily
life / by Robert Corin Morris.
        p. cm.
    ISBN: 0-358-0985-4
    1. Spiritual life.   I. Title.
    BV4501.3 M674   2003
    248.4–dc21
2002013578
                    Printed in the United States of America

Try me, O God,
and seek the ground of my heart;
prove me, and examine my thoughts. . . .
and lead me in the way everlasting.

—Psalm 139:23-24 (1928 BCP)

CONTENTS

ACKNOWLEDGMENTS

I am deeply grateful to all the people over the years who have badgered me to put some of my teaching into a book. As a teacher, preacher, and speaker who uses notes, not manuscripts, and often "wings it," capturing these thoughts in a net and getting them on a page does not come naturally. Julie Wortman, a former editor of *The Witness,* was the first adviser who took the time to teach me how to convert my breezy, extemporaneous style to publishable prose.

Since then I've had many helpers, including John Mogabgab and the gracious staff of *Weavings: A Journal of the Christian Spiritual Life* (Nashville: Upper Room Ministries), in which a version of chapters 1, 7–11, and 16 first appeared. A variety of manuscript readers, including David and Janet Bate, David Bate Jr., Robert Festa, James Wangbickler, and Tom Rieber offered valuable feedback. Lisa Green, assistant director at Interweave, Inc., proved a skilled wordsmith and critical editor. Veronica Escalona labored over footnotes and the copy machine. JoAnn Miller and Jeannie Crawford-Lee at Upper Room Books were astute in their critiques and warmly supportive at all stages of the editorial process.

I am also indebted to the many people whose stories are recounted here. Learning from the experiences of others is the most rewarding part of being a pastor and teacher. Where individuals' names are used straightforwardly, it is with their permission. Others have asked to remain anonymous. Still other stories come from people whom I could not possibly now contact. In those cases, identifying characteristics and circumstances have been changed, but the story line is true to their experience.

Most of all, my wife of over thirty years, Suzanne, was, as usual, a sounding board, graciously humorous critic, and constant support.

PART I

Opening to Grace

The real state of our spiritual life is best revealed late on some Tuesday or Thursday afternoon, after a rough day. Mountaintop raptures are all well and good, even necessary, but what happens in the valley has long-lasting results in our lives and the lives of those we meet.

I like to imagine that Jesus' disciples had a rough day when James and John decided the best way to handle a snub from the nearby Samaritan village was asking Jesus to destroy the inhabitants by calling down fire from heaven. Jesus neither scolded James and John nor called down fire from heaven. I don't know whether he felt like laughing or crying, so little had the two disciples grasped his teaching. Jesus did confront them with a piercing observation: "You do not know what kind of spirit you are of, for the Son of Man did not come to destroy . . . but to save" (Luke 9:56, NIV).[1] He challenged them to reflect on the motions of their own hearts, to learn the art of knowing their own spirits.

Knowing our own spirits is the issue for all our encounters: In "what kind of spirit" do we face our coworkers, our friends or partners, our children, strangers, opponents, even our pets in the middle of a rough day? I don't imagine God expects us always to respond calmly and lovingly, but I've come to believe God wants us to develop awareness of the state of our spirit, for our own sake and the sake of others. And I've come to know that God can begin molding any spirit, however cranky, toward better ends than we would devise for ourselves.

11

CHAPTER 1

The Second Breath

Frustration as a Doorway to Spiritual Practice

I didn't begin praying in a steady, daily way until I gave up all attempts to develop a "prayer life." I'd tried a number of schemes to implement regular daily spiritual practice over the years. But sooner or later the force of daily habit reasserted itself, and, like a sand castle, my nicely regularized "prayer life" would dissolve into the high tide of my reactions to the unpredictable course of each day's happenings. Life was just too pressured, too episodic, too unpredictable to carve out the space necessary for satisfying prayer.

Then one day, rushing behind schedule from one activity to another, I stubbed my toe on the stairs, breathed a frustrated curse—and suddenly realized that I was praying! Not that a curse makes a very good prayer; it's rather poor-spirited, in fact. But ornery as it was, it was nonetheless a kind of prayer, groaning its way from the heart of my hassled, pressured self. The clue to the curse's prayerfulness was that it actually began with the words "O God!"—followed by some rather colorful wishes.

"O God"? . . . I mused, toe still throbbing. *That's a prayer! Well, if I'm praying, why not go all the way?* So on the next conscious breath, I breathed more deeply and repeated, in a somewhat more friendly groan, "O God!" On the third breath I heard myself pray, with more feeling, "O God . . . bless." That one word *bless* evoked a cascade of feelings: *Bless my aching toe,*

bless my ruffled spirits, bless my frazzled body . . . bless me in my heed-less rush. . . .

The next breath brought with it an imagistic prayer honed in those periodic attempts at "prayer life"—the warm light of God gracefully suffusing my body, soothing my soul. The adrenaline surge of frustration receded, the toe throbbed its way into a healing ache, and my mind noted that the search for a daily prayer discipline had finally found the place to set up practice—right in the heartland of daily frustration itself. Our first breath of frustration may be filled with a curse, but we determine the future by what we do with the second breath. That day, accepting frustration as an understandable reaction rather than rejecting it allowed the frustration to begin learning how to breathe more deeply into grace, instead of spiraling into deeper unhappiness and cursing. "We breathe, expand, and let go, and something comes in from elsewhere."[1]

BLESSING, NOT CURSING

As I began to use this approach to whatever irked me, I noted how this second-breath moment is a crucial pivot between cursing and blessing. The wisdom of Scripture sets out a clear choice to be made: "I have set before you life and death, blessings and curses. Choose life so that you . . . may live" (Deut. 30:19). The choice we make powerfully affects the spirit we bring to any encounter. For me, that day on the stairs, an event-based daily spiritual practice had begun.

The impact of our "spiritual life," after all, has to do with the spirit in which we approach people and events. That spirit displays itself as much in the moments of frustration as in the moments of inspiration. As we stew in reactive emotions, we are engaging in "spiritual practice," however unhelpful, which affects our presence to ourselves and others. The way we live our life is our spiritual practice—no more, no less, nothing but, nothing else.

Frustration presents a particularly rich place to set up daily spiritual practice because it occurs in the rub between our lofty idealizations and our actual, knee-jerk reactions. Frustration is where our human spirits practice dealing with life as it arises to meet us, rather than as we'd arrange things if we were God. A moment of frustration is a real relationship between soul and life rather than a moment of idealized spiritual fantasy and protected exaltation. A good place to begin.

In such a clash our frustrated, reactive selves often rule the roost, coloring the spirit of the encounter—whether it be with the stairs, the opponent, the coworker, the friend, the broken toy, the malfunctioning machine, the dumb fool on the finance committee, the jerk who just cut us off on the freeway, the idiot who . . . and so it goes, when it really gets going. Frustration bends the muscles of our faces, shapes our words, moans inside our tone of voice, spreads in an acrid biochemical stew throughout our flesh, and sprays out from us like an infectious cloud. That's spiritual power!

The Bible calls this groaning, moaning, frustrated sputtering reactivity "cursing," and it happens easily, quite apart from any four-letter words we may or may not use. The Hebrew root of the word for curse has to do with restraining and binding, a diminishment of spirit. It is the opposite of blessing, which implies letting be, enrichment, expansion of spirit.[2]

Cursing is an attitude in action. It includes all our ways of seeking power and good feelings by diminishing the opposition. Surprised, crossed, or opposed, we reach out for aid to bolster our threatened spirits with implicit or explicit invocations of spirit-power. We use all the tools of spiritual practice, however unwittingly: word, image, ritual gesture, invocation. We may utter crude power-words to cut the threat down to size or wordlessly dismiss the intrusive event with an animal sound: a snort, a sniff, or a "harrumph!" The hand may move in ritually expressive power to threaten or dismiss; the lips curl in disgust; the lips tighten, and the teeth bare in an unconscious showing of our fangs. Behind it all lies a dark rumination of a universe gone sinister, requiring power to resist or triumph: "Why does this always . . . ?" "Why doesn't it ever . . . ?" "Isn't that just the way!" "By God, I'll—" Those difficult cursing passages from the Prophets and the Psalms speak with vivid honesty of our common human feelings in moments of frustration: "Why did I come forth from the womb to see toil and sorrow?" (Jer. 20:18) or "Let their habitation be desolate; . . . let them be blotted out of the book of the living" (Ps. 69:25, 28, KJV). Psalm 69 is the most vivid of biblical curses, which were a conscious, time-honored, common spiritual practice. Jesus' prohibition of cursing and call to replace cursing with its more powerful twin, blessing, directly challenged a thriving religious ritual—now practiced mostly unconsciously.

Perhaps Scripture presents these bloodcurdling passages to make us more conscious of our sometimes sinister reactions to daily events. We may, of course, feel ashamed and curse ourselves for cursing—sending these natural reactions into oblivion until the next time they erupt. Or we can accept frustration as a signal that our soul and life are really engaged with each other! Recognizing the impulse to curse as the impulse to pray, however imperfectly, helps us bless our reactivity rather than stuff it back in the dark closet. We can view our frustrated moans as part of creation's "groaning" for new and better life, yearning for the renewing power of God's grace, rather than as barriers.[3]

We face a stark choice: Will we bless our life as it arises—inside us as well as outside us—or curse it? Bless ourselves or curse ourselves?[4] That day when my stubbed toe's pain leaped to my lips as a curse, I was graced to let that groan find a larger space to breathe in. Like a hurt child turning to its mother, my wounded spirit reached out for a blessing, setting human pain in its true homeland—the presence of grace, God's active goodness in and through any situation. Jesus lived in such a state of mind, one in which every "enemy," however small, was blessed rather than cursed. When we live with this attitude, the desire to do good becomes the basis for whatever practical strategy we adopt toward a difficulty or problem: "Love your enemies, . . . bless those who curse you" (Luke 6:27-28). Jesus, it seems, even tells us how to practice that love: do good, pray for, and give, rather than react, curse, and withhold.

OCCASIONS FOR PRACTICE

Once I saw frustration as an invitation to breathe more deeply into grace, the occasions for spiritual practice multiplied rapidly.

I'm late setting out to teach a class, twenty minutes away by car. As I barrel down the street, I'm emotionally pushing, urging the car forward in a nonverbal, almost magical inner compulsion. It's the same irrational impulse that makes me push elevator buttons more than once, vainly urging the entirely automatic creatures to speed up. As luck or the perversity of life (there goes the cosmic story spinning itself out) would have it, I not only hit every red light, but I get behind a school bus. My emotional magic pushes harder, grunting and groaning against obstacles: *Why does it always happen like this . . . ? No wait . . . remember . . . just "O God" will do.* As the moan becomes a real prayer, a crystal-clear thought laces through my upset: *The harder you push at things, the harder they push back!* I don't really believe I'm creating my own external reality, but I am creating an internal story of great obstacles that's making me frustrated. *Deep breath. Don't push. O God! Here, now . . . sunlight through leaves . . . child smiling from back of bus . . . goodness everywhere.* My state of mind when I arrive to teach becomes much more important than being five minutes late.

This method—letting frustration become prayer, giving pain or anger or misery a graceful space in which to breathe—resembles a highly effective mind-body medical treatment for chronic pain sufferers.[5] Patients combine their drug therapy with appropriate exercises and a startling meditative method. This method invites them to let the pain itself be the focal point for the meditation. Not attempting to make it go away. Just letting it be. Letting the pain fill the awareness without "cursing" it, cringing against it, seeking to block it out.

As people focus gently on their breathing, letting their mind dwell on only one thing, the simple sensation of the pain, both mind and body stop pushing in tension against the enemy; the muscles begin to relax, actually lessening the pain. More importantly, the field of awareness becomes more spacious, big enough to contain both the pain and other matters. For many, the pain becomes bearable with less medication and becomes a companion rather than a competitor for attention. These folk are learning to bless, not curse in a most basic way.

As Kathleen Norris suggests, "The point of our crises and calamities is not to frighten us or beat us into submission but to encourage us to change, to allow us to heal and grow."[6] Are the uncontrollables, the unpredictables of life, the harsher reactions of our souls the enemies or the occasions of our spiritual practice? We don't need to resist our knee-jerk, first-breath responses! We just keep taking every occasion to the second breath, the breath of blessing. We are redeemed more by setting our distempers in God's sunlight than by resisting the dark, shadow side of our natures. Perhaps this provides one clue to the meaning of Jesus' strange admonition, "Resist not evil" (Matt. 5:39, KJV).

AWAKE TO THE PRESENT MOMENT

What starts as a kind of spiritual stress management technique can free us progressively from preoccupation with our reactive self. Then our hearts can reach out for the goodness available in every moment and become more alert to the call of grace in any situation.

Someone is late for an appointment with me. Do I curse his alleged ineptitude and claim this as an inconvenience—or turn the time to good use? Someone asks my help when I'm already headed to help someone else. Do I make a knee-jerk, willful response or take a second breath and ask the Spirit what may be called for here, now? A newspaper story socks me in the gut with an outrage. Do I go into a dither, cluck my way toward righteous anger, or hold the people I'm reading about in my heart for a moment of blessing and intercession? Gradually the day becomes peppered with prayer.

It helps, of course, to have a variety of prayer-aids or invocations to go with that second breath. For me, useful techniques include staying focused on the breath; picturing an image of light radiating from the heart and suffusing the body; humming a chant phrase while singing the words in my mind; and, most of all, the simple body prayer of an upturned palm. All these practices, honed in periodic episodes of spiritual discipline, become useful in the moment.

I stand behind a tangibly impatient woman at the local bakery. A dozen customers wait ahead of us, and fewer salesclerks than usual assist them. The woman sighs; she huffs; she shifts restlessly from one foot to another, checking the time. Her frustration agitates the air around her.

She may have a right to be impatient for all I know. No doubt she had not planned to spend her time this way. We can stand on our rights all the way to hell and back, for all the good it will do. But this ten minutes of life will never come again for either of us. The choice right now is between the heavenly and the hellish.

My own annoyance takes a deep second breath. As my right hand turns palm up in an unobtrusive gesture of prayer, the sights and sounds of this friendly bakery become clearer. Two small children play in the nearby kiddie corner. Sunlight streams through the window behind me, warming my back. It's a wonderful place to be on a busy Saturday morning, full of wholesome goodness. My favorite Hebrew chant, *Hineni* ("Here am I"), arises in the back of my throat. The gift of standing here is simple, good, and sweet. I share that goodness with the unhappy woman, surrounding her with God's light in my heart. I can't say this makes much difference in her behavior, but it's better than my impatience rubbing against her impatience. She treats the salesclerk with snippy sarcasm, which I at least am able to soothe when my turn comes. The saleswoman smiles.

Since "all human souls . . . are interconnected,"[7] the state of our souls has a ripple effect on those around us. Who knows what pressures affect the saleswoman? Will my annoyance add to the unknown burdens she carries, spilling out in her own reactivity to partner or children? The presence we bring to every encounter has incalculable results. The prayer of the second breath concerns not only, or even primarily, me. It is about the world.

Difficulties don't disappear. In fact, they may multiply. If one prays for patience, wouldn't it make sense that occasions to practice patience might increase? that even more deeply ingrained reactive patterns might surface, groaning their way toward grace?

Feelings of frustration don't magically turn into golden glows of cheerfulness every time I remember to practice the second-breath prayer. Far from it! But I've learned to keep from spiraling deeper into diminishment. Episodes of orneriness and grimness, irritability and ill-temperedness indicate losing touch with a "state of grace," to use that remarkably apt old Catholic phrase. Being an agent of that grace is surely our most important contribution in any situation.

I sit, late at night, in the Summit, New Jersey, train station, alone except for a half-dozen boisterous African-American teenage boys with a boom box. Their loud joking seems to have an angry undercurrent. The knee-jerk racist responses of a fifty-six-year-old white man run in the background. I feel slightly apprehensive: *I wish I weren't alone here; I resent their noise taking up all the public space: Why do they always have to . . . ? Wish you'd pipe down! Wish your pushy self-assertiveness were diminished!*

Diminished? My soul wakes up from the grumbling reverie. I'm inwardly cursing them! I take the second breath, turning the inner disturbance toward God. The adrenaline arousal lessens, and the mind opens to the moment. I try to discern the true nature of their mood. It dawns on me that they are just having a good time. The boom box, the loudness, the physical boisterousness reflect, quite innocently, age, class, and cultural differences.

Then a thought laces through me: *These kids must constantly be on the receiving end of white disapproval like mine.* I can imagine what it's like to be looked at, felt at, that way. I've been in situations where I just didn't fit—or fitted some stereotype all too well. *Dear God! Turn me and I shall be turned.* I turn to blessing, and a new daily practice is born: a heart-blessing for people who are different from me, especially those whose means of expression rub against the grain of my own.

Another chance to practice soon presents itself. On the train a few days later I sit down a space away from a woman who is aggressively devouring an egg roll. She gives me a look of annoyance and turns her head away to concentrate on dipping her roll in soy sauce, which splatters about as generously as her obvious unhappiness and anger. Just what I need with this tan raincoat on!

Annoyance and compassion wrestle in my body and mind.

Each encounter we have is part of our daily offering to God. Each day, every deed, all the intentional motion of our souls—however helpful or hurtful it may be—is the actual "living sacrifice" we give to God as material with which to weave the human story (see Rom. 12:1). At this daily altar our selves are offered to or withheld from the Spirit's transforming power. Rituals, retreats, and formal worship—essential as they are to nourish us, orient us toward God, and train us in spiritual exercises—merely prepare us for real meetings at the altar of particular moments.

The grace of a number of second breaths allowed the impulse toward compassion win out over annoyance: I held the woman eating the egg roll in compassionate light in my heart. I observed that her agitation actually began to lessen. She took a deep breath. Her hand rattled the paper bag loudly as she rummaged about in it.

"Hey! Mister," rang in my right ear. I turned to look at her. "You wanna egg roll?" She shoved it across the space between us. "I don't wannit. You wannit?" No, I didn't much want it;

but yes, indeed, I did! I took the offered piece of grace and savored every bite.

For practices to center and focus consciousness, see Exercises 1–3 in the appendix.

CHAPTER 2

Available Grace

Invoking God's blessing in moments of frustration opens our consciousness to a vast pool of blessing that surrounds us, mostly unnoticed, at all times. God is all-pervasive, and yet we live, mostly, impervious to the flow of grace. As a friend puts it, "Sure, God is everywhere, for all the good it will do you." He means no irreverence. He knows that there's a big difference between thinking "God is everywhere" and cultivating what Christians call a "realized sense of the Presence." The challenge is not getting God into our lives but realizing that our lives are already in God. Such a realization is more difficult for a mind constantly reactive to life's frustrations. It is easier for a mind that has learned how to be present in the moment, receptive to what comes.

CULTIVATING A HABITUAL RECEPTIVITY TO GRACE

One modern psychiatrist describes the transition from reactivity to receptivity as a shift from "instrumental" consciousness to "connectedness."[1] In the instrumental mode we relate to things and people according to our fears and desires, and we manipulate things and people for our own purposes: survival, pleasure, and meaning. The connective state of mind, on the other hand, is receptive rather than instrumental. In it we relate deeply rather than manipulatively. In this alternative organization of our consciousness, we connect to the realities beyond our ego-borders. Rather than critiquing and analyzing reality, we welcome it. We become more open to the stirrings of our own souls, the distinct reality of other souls, and the fabric of the world.

Our whole being literally expands in connectedness, all the way from a slight easing of tension to a deep mystical rapport with God-pervaded reality. This natural state of mind serves as the doorway to what the New Testament calls "walking in the Spirit" and Christian tradition calls "a state of grace." Unfortunately we continually forfeit our spiritual birthright of connectedness by getting lost in reactivity, becoming mean-spirited, and then doing harm to ourselves and to others.

The very existence of these two different organizations of consciousness in our nature signifies that our body is "wired for God," as Dr. Herbert Benson of Harvard Medical School puts it.[2] Human nature itself yearns for the shift toward grace and has the ability to turn toward it. This shift can happen spontaneously, as in those moments when we are entranced by love or beauty.

Children spend much of their time in a state of connective consciousness since they have built up fewer layers of fretful reactivity and resistance than adults and are easily lured into moments of wonder, love, and praise. In the spiritual sharing groups I lead, I have heard more than one story of childhood awakening to God.

When only four, while playing in the shade of a tree in her yard, Eileen suddenly found herself in a pool of sunlight. In that moment, it wasn't just sunlight but something more; and she was filled with awe, wonder, and love. "My whole being just knew that this, This was God. This was what they talked about in church, but It was different and more wonderful." She lay there, like a cat in the sun, communing with the Mystery.

Jean came to a similar realization in a tomato field at about the same age. The hot sun, the black soil, the pungent smell of the vines above her head, loud buzzing of insects, the lush redness of the ripe tomatoes overwhelmed her senses and lifted the experience to something larger. There had to be "Something Magnificent" behind and within all this aliveness. She felt awed by the beauty and energy pouring through the scene and pulling her into it. When she began attending Lutheran Sunday school, she recognized what her teachers were talking about when they said, "God is great, God is good." She had experienced this connection with divine Presence and been thrilled by it. Her later experience of that Presence in confirmation and Holy Communion felt wholly affirming, familiar, and authentic to her.

We need not expect such experiences as the substance of daily spiritual life, any more than we expect moments of ecstasy as the bread and butter of personal relationships. But those experiences do perform an important function: they reveal the constant, all-pervasive presence of the Divine. Grace is as available as the air we breathe. The divine Presence surrounds us just as substantially as the air. As Scripture puts it, "We live and move and have our being" (Acts 17:28) in God just as the fish of the sea swim in water—*whether we're noticing it or not.*

Maybe Jesus encourages us to become "as a little child" (Luke 18:17) because children make this shift into connectedness more easily. For adults, cultivating such an easy childlike shift takes practice.

LEARNING TO BE PRESENT TO BLESSING

My sudden insight about turning curse into blessing actually represented the culmination of a process that had been going on for many years. Recurrent struggle to find a daily spiritual routine had led me to practice various spiritual arts with intensity for short-lived periods. Now, with my insight, these arts became available to me in a new way, to bring daily life—rough edges and all—kicking and screaming, if need be, into the light of blessing.

The first major practice I had explored was mindfulness, cultivated through centering meditation that focuses here and now on only one thing at a time. At the beginning, I had simply let my breathing focus my attention. Over time my wandering mind could rest simply on the flow of the breath. Then I could turn my focus in any direction: toward beholding a flower, tasting an apple, listening deeply to another person, or simply being fully present in any moment. I could easily convert this meditation practice into a "breath prayer" of intentional openness to the Divine.

The second practice was what spiritual healer Agnes Sanford called "harnessing the imagination" in prayer, visualizing the presence of God as a healing light surrounding me or bathing another person. I had become accustomed to evoking the inward image of light and imagining it pervading a situation, even when my eyes were open.[3]

Mostly I had practiced these spiritual disciplines in times apart from the unpredictable flow of daily life—on vacation, in times of leisure or great enjoyment. The third major practice, the Jewish art of saying *berakot*, blessings for any good thing encountered, I learned during one of the bleakest periods of my early adulthood. During a time of extended depression, this prayer habit had been a lifesaver, no less. It didn't make everything wonderful, but the practice did help keep me in touch with some sense of reality in the midst of the muddled, swirling, bleak feelings.

This practice invites us to be on the lookout for signs of the divine Goodness in the most ordinary stuff of life: the first breath of the morning, the nourishment of each meal, taste, touch, beauty, acts of kindness, good thoughts. Once discovered, such signs can be acknowledged with simple "arrow prayers," such as "Blessed art Thou, O Lord our God, King of the Universe, who . . . created the fruit of the vine . . . created such beauty . . . has given this wisdom." The tradition delights in creating prayers for every occasion, including difficult ones. When the rabbi in *Fiddler on the Roof* is asked whether there is an appropriate blessing for the czar, he thinks a moment and intones, "God bless and keep the Czar—far away from us!"

I had learned that this practice of blessing has also been deeply woven into Christianity. The early Celtic church, rooted as it was in Middle Eastern Christian practice, pulsed with endless variations on the blessing theme, blessing God for every sight, odor, taste, song note, and ray of guidance, through which "the zeal that seeks" our living souls comes into our lives.[4]

What began as words of blessing led to a deeper savoring of all the different qualities of goodness present in any moment, no matter how bad everything else seemed: taking just a moment to savor the pleasure of someone's smile, sunlight through leaves, the taste of a strawberry, the relaxing waterfall of warm water on the shoulders while taking a shower, the sudden surprise of an insight, the camaraderie of a dinner party, the good energy of a gathering of people. As time went on, this practice began helping me see afresh what hadn't seemed like blessings before: the shades of gray in a cloudy winter sky, the exquisite lines of leafless trees against that gray backdrop, the pastel colors of midwinter, the invigorating quality of cold. I began to experience what Tilden Edwards calls the "graced edge" of any situation.[5]

Before I began to practice *berakot*, this practice of blessing God, moments of goodness had to reach out and grab me dramatically. The practice of blessing retrained my senses to notice elements in the landscape of life I previously passed by heedlessly. This new awareness fed my soul and slowly reshaped my attitudes. Simple goodness, savored, more and more became an experience of being blessed by a Goodness that always had been lurking in things, unnoticed and hidden.

I could now invoke this Goodness in blessing upon the rough edges of life, calling upon the presence of the Spirit to pervade any situation. On the stairs that day, toe hurting, I had brought meditative awareness of the pain together with the art of blessing and discovered that the two provided a powerful opening to the presence of God.

CULTIVATING A GOD-ROOTED CONSCIOUSNESS

All spiritual traditions have developed methods of *ascesis*, the discipline or training of both body and consciousness toward living more habitually in this connective level. The methods involve a host of spiritual exercises that give muscle to our intention to turn toward grace. All involve techniques of helping the total self—mind, body, and spirit—make the shift from ego-bound to connective consciousness. Some methods have hovered at the margins of Western Christian practice or been forgotten entirely. Only recently have they been rediscovered and gained increasing acceptance.

These methods of mind training are a vital part of what the Hebrew Scriptures call *teshuva* or "turning" to God. When translated as "repentance," as it usually is, this word seems to suggest that we start focusing on our own faults, inadequacies, sins, and failings; whereas it is, quite simply, an invitation to turn away from self-preoccupation toward available grace. The same can be said for the New Testament word *metanoia*—literally, "going beyond your (present) state of mind." Turn your whole self— faults, strengths, everything—toward grace: go beyond your present state of mind; the active presence and rule of God are at hand. Look, see, claim, receive—now.

This "turning" is neither a once-in-a-lifetime event nor a lifelong preoccupation with sin. Turning toward God involves a continual, habitually recurring shift from an ego-driven agenda to a receptive openness to grace, from fretful reactivity to the welcoming breath of blessing. The Benedictines call this practice "a continual conversion of the heart."[6]

Some traditional methods of Christian mind cultivation include the following:

SIMPLE TURNING

Perhaps the most widespread example of this practice is the use of "arrow prayers" like the one I claimed on the staircase with my stubbed toe: "O my God!" In any moment one can employ a short phrase to turn the mind toward grace and remember the presence of God. I have come to call this practice "simple turning." A person claims a short prayer phrase, mental image, or memory of closeness to God to call upon many times during the day. The individual may link this conscious expression to everyday activities—washing hands, entering a new situation, beginning a snack or meal, pushing back from the desk for a break, taking a deep breath. When I linked arrow prayers to moments of frustration, a transformative breakthrough occurred.

SIMPLE FOCUS

For centuries people of all faiths have used the universal practice of breath awareness described earlier to evoke a shift in mind and body toward relaxed focus and alert receptivity. In Christian practice, we direct this openness intentionally toward the grace of God as known in Christ. This kind of prayer formed the backbone of spiritual practice for the Desert Fathers and Mothers in the early Christian centuries and continued to be prominent in medieval contemplative prayer. Adherents of Eastern Orthodox faith still practice this prayer style in the popular "Jesus Prayer." In recent years, Thomas Keating's Centering Prayer movement has reintroduced the breath prayer to Western Christians.[7] I stumbled on this prayer form when I learned to focus on my breathing during meditation. Even my own haphazard practice of it through the years had helped me learn the "feel" of the shift from an instrumental to a connective state of mind.

Having taught this form of prayer to hundreds of people over the years, I still marvel at the subtle changes that occur in people's faces, even in the atmosphere of the room, when a group of people practices this prayer together in silence for ten or fifteen minutes. The hard lines of the faces soften, mouths often turn up in a gentle smile, and the busy mental energy of the room quietens into a stillness. Little wonder. We're doing something the body yearns for, according to medical studies. The biochemical factories in the brain pump out neurotransmitters and enzymes that soothe and repair the body and smooth the prickly places in the emotions. This natural grace, while not in and of itself prayer, invites us to a state of consciousness in which the heart and mind can focus more easily, if they choose, on God. One priest who experienced this kind of quiet focus at a seminar said that it was the "missing first base" in his prayer life. A layman at a training conference, when asked what he'd learned, blurted out that he "had never realized prayer was actually a way to invite the Spirit into a meeting."

My favorite incident of group meditative prayer occurred during a church service one Sunday morning. During the sermon time, I had led the congregation in Centering Prayer, concluding the ten-minute silence by reciting the Lord's Prayer slowly and intentionally. Afterward people commented that they had said that prayer as if they "had never heard the words before." Two elderly sisters came out beaming. "That was wonderful," they said. "The church was so still you could hear the silence," said one. "It was more than just silence," said her sister. "It was quiet enough to feel God." They both nodded vigorously. "It was different, you know. Wonderful. Not at all like church, of course." They meant that church services often clatter along in instrumental consciousness, talking at God and preaching at people, but offer little help in fostering receptivity to God in the moment.

IMAGINAL PRAYER

In the first form of a centering-type prayer I learned, I imagined myself surrounded by the light of God and sitting quietly in its glow. Since a picture is worth a thousand words, why not pray in pictures? Episcopalian spiritual healer Agnes Sanford recommended this approach as the first step in her healing prayer practice. She believed that, for some people at least, a picture held in the imagination kept the mind steady better than a word or words. Brain research reveals that our minds are always responding to life not only with thoughts but also with images, feelings, and body sensations as well as concepts. Thus imaginal prayer involves the whole incarnate person, attuning heart, mind, and body to the Spirit. The great medieval Jewish thinker Maimonides described the "imaginative faculties" as crucial to developing an "intuitive" sense of God and claimed that knowledge of God comes more from imagination than from intellect alone.[8] Such practices are rooted in the wisdom of the ages.

The use of mental images in prayer has a long history in biblically based spirituality. Grounded in the Jewish mystical practice that came before it, Christianity was open to dream and vision, to using intentional images as a way of focusing heart and mind on God's grace. The New Testament speaks of envisioning Christ throned in triumph in the heavens (Col. 3:1), the disciple surrounded by an "armor of light" (Rom. 13:12), and God's light shining "in our hearts" (2 Cor. 4:6). I have come to believe these phrases may refer to actual prayer practices. Saint Augustine entered into the world of images to find God.[9] Periodically forgotten and then revived—as in Saint Ignatius's famous Spiritual Exercises—imaginal prayer is experiencing powerful renewal in our own era.

This form of prayer isn't "just in your imagination," as if you were making things up. One of the fundamental ways the brain processes information takes place through imaging. Our imaginal responses to any experience are as real as thinking about it in words. And, like words, images can sometimes take wings, opening into something beyond themselves.

For years I used an imaginal prayer in which I saw the light of God radiating from deep within my heart, suffusing my whole being. This prayer carried me through times of depression and always buoyed my spirits, however slightly. It continually affirmed my belief that God's light was shining, even in the darkness. One day during a time of pivotal transition in my life, I turned to this prayer form as to an old friend, expecting nothing more than the reassurance of this affirmation. As I formed the image of light in my heart, something happened: my mentally constructed image dissolved, and a clear, warm, palpable golden Light filled the center of my chest, radiating with a virtually three-dimensional quality, shining with Love. *O my God*, I thought. *Can this be real?* Tears came to my eyes as this warmth permeated my body with the kind of stinging, soothing warmth a sip of wine makes as it courses through the body's interior. With this warmth came the conviction that God was indeed with me in this time of transition and that I could trust God's guidance.

I've not had such a dramatic experience of light since then, but every time I use the light image in prayer, something of the glow lingers on. I know I am imaging something utterly real.[10] Such images can powerfully deepen the "arrow prayers" used for targeted moments during the day. In group prayer settings, a common image often becomes the doorway to a common experience of "shift" into a deeper state of prayer and a profound sense of the Spirit's manifestation.

CHANTS AND CHORUSES

More familiar, ordinary religious practices employ music to alter consciousness and enchant heart and mind. The repeated choruses or praise songs used in evangelical and charismatic circles, the sung refrains for psalms now popular in churches, and the forms of ancient chant being practiced by many people engender the shift to connective receptivity. The ecumenical monks of Taizé, France, have crafted a deeply moving, modern, polyphonic form of repeated chants, which is gaining popularity. Like the other prayer forms, chants and choruses give the wandering mind a place to return and invite the "relaxation response," a doorway to grace for the willing heart.

Such chanting does not have to be communal. An individual can sing any short prayer phrase in a monotone or simple invented melody and carry it throughout the day. At moments when the mind finishes its work on a thought, the inner chant becomes the fallback place for heart and mind. I find myself inwardly turning to such chant phrases in moments of frustration.

But for many of us, nothing equals group singing. I'll never forget a literal "mountaintop" experience with chant among three hundred Episcopal college students one New Year's Eve in the Rockies. As Communion was served at our midnight service, we sang a haunting repeated chant in canon, with words drawn from the Song of Moses (Deut. 32), picturing God as a mother eagle hovering over her nest, spreading out her wings to enfold us. The music was lovely, yes; certainly the crowd was "really psyched," as one student put it. The chant definitely put us all in a mellow mood. But something more happened. Like the Light coming into my mentally constructed image of light, Something More filled the chant. "It just took off," said a colleague. "It was like somebody took the roof off and we were under the vastness of the sky," said another. "We became absolutely one body, one heart, one mind," said yet another. "We dropped out of time," declared the celebrant. It was as if waves of Love washed over the group. Slowly, slowly the chant stopped, followed by a profound silence "so deep it felt as if you could hear it," according to another student. The crowd that had been "psyched up" with youthful enthusiasm sat quiet and still, deeply absorbed in an awareness of quiet, discernible Presence pervading and connecting the hundreds of worshipers. After a long while, the music combo began softly playing, bringing everyone back into the familiar concluding prayers of the Eucharist.

THE MIND OF CHRIST

Slowly but surely we can cultivate the habits of mind and heart that put us in touch with the "mind of Christ," that is, the spirit in which he dealt with the rough edges of human experience. Our lives, like his, are meant to be carried along in the steady flow of the Spirit of God. And surely, for Jesus, *practicing the presence of God* keeps him available to that flow.

Jesus insists that grace is available for the asking. God's gracious presence and active ruling power are "pressing at the gates" of our lives (Matt. 3:2, RCM). Neither ritual requirements nor personal worthiness stands in the way. God will "give the Holy Spirit" and with that Spirit, "good things" to "those who ask" (Matt. 7:11; Luke 11:13). The Good News promises that the grace manifested in Christ is available to the trusting, open heart (see Gal. 2:16). All that is required is the receiving. And that takes a bit of practice.

To practice mindfulness, see Exercise 1, item 5 in the appendix. For other practices to fill consciousness with blessing and compassion, see Exercises 2–5 and 7.

CHAPTER 3

Meeting Grace on Its Own Terms

If we want to meet the Divine on its own terms, we need to be receptive to what's there, not what we think is supposed to be there. I once heard a monk who had spent thirty years in a contemplative order say wistfully and somewhat bitterly that he had "never had an encounter with God." *What was he expecting,* I wondered. Perhaps he was looking for something too exalted: a visionary experience or the vivid sense that he was in the tangible presence of a Person. Such visitations do happen but not in the course of most everyday lives.

We can easily go through life waiting to run into some predetermined idea or experience of God, completely missing the actual ways the Divine encounters us in every moment. Looking too high, we miss what's here on the ground alongside us. Looking for some highly anticipated face of God, we may miss the face that's looking at us right now.

Jesus tells us emphatically that the Divine is available, but he gives no assurance that we can determine in advance in exactly what form the Spirit will appear to us. We need to cultivate an increasing openness to the manifold faces, guises, and even disguises this One Mysterious Reality may use to manifest its presence and communicate its grace to us.

Had that bitter contemplative monk never been surprised by a sudden joy, never known an unexpected moment of peace, never given thanks for some small goodness, never stopped to notice the enchantment of beauty? Had his spiritual director never asked him to consider that his very longing for God was a "sigh" of the Spirit within him "too deep for words" (Rom. 8:26)?

THE QUALITIES OF GRACE

The monk might better have begun by savoring the qualities of everyday experience. One of my favorite spiritual masters Brother Lawrence was a seventeenth-century monk who despaired of finding God when his superiors put him on permanent kitchen duty. Then he realized that it was in the ordinary tasks of the kitchen that he was meant to find, and be found by, God's love.

The practice of blessing God for ordinary goodness taught me how to savor the many qualities at work in any given situation— qualities in my own body and soul and qualities in the surrounding people and environment. Then the second-breath practice taught me that I could choose what quality or aspect of the Spirit's presence I needed to call upon for any particular situation.

I was happy to discover that my self-taught practice was, in fact, grounded in the long history of Jewish and Christian spirituality. That tradition views the play of gracious qualities at work in any situation as the outcroppings of a myriad of divine "energies" always at work throughout creation. The ancient vision of the Eastern Orthodox Church emphasizes how God becomes known through these "infinite and eternal energies" rushing in "movements" through the world, streams of grace "in which everything that exists participates." Grace is present, shining and available in every situation to eyes that can see it, waiting to be savored, named, and claimed. The conscious claiming we call prayer fosters connection with these energies, "making the greatness of God to shine forth in all things."[1]

This Christian insight stems from an even older Hebrew vision. Jewish mystical interpretation of the Bible knows these energies as "names" of God—all the many different attributes or aspects that make up the divine character. Chief among those traditional attributes are Wisdom, Understanding, Loving-kindness, Judgment, Mercy, Beauty, Endurance, Majesty, Creativity, and Sovereignty,[2] though the list varies from teacher to teacher. These are not the names of some distant being but dynamic spiritual forces flowing from the heart of God that shape the world—qualities that are echoed in the human soul. All the names make up the one Great, Unspeakable Name of God. When we say "hallowed be thy Name," we call on the living presence of God sounding throughout creation.

These attributes are also manifested in the metaphorical word images that dot the pages of Scripture and well up from the depths of our own souls. The image of God in human beings is meant to resonate with these images. Our state of consciousness can be altered decisively by calling upon a name of God lovingly, pondering an attribute or quality of the divine nature or opening ourselves to a particular aspect of the divine energies. We are designed to grow, slowly, from "one degree of glory to another" as we allow God's own Spirit to have its way with our spirits (2 Cor. 3:18).

HUMAN QUALITIES AND THE EXPERIENCE OF GRACE

Godlike qualities at work in the human spirit are the most intimate and ordinary ways the Spirit becomes manifest. "Love, joy, peace, patience, kindness, generosity, faithfulness, gentleness, and self-control" in human nature are the fruit of the Spirit of God's manifold qualities at work in us (Gal. 5:22-23). If the eyes of our soul are truly opened to God, we begin to see the divine energies at work in all the seemingly ordinary qualities of life. Because God is the Source of all things, every genuine goodness is rooted in a deeper Goodness. The ordinary experiences of peace or beauty or love can be more clearly seen as the presence of Peace, Beauty, or Love; we realize that the "ordinary" is not only infinitely precious but also inexhaustibly rooted in deep Mystery. The qualities that operate in nature and human nature begin to appear "with their capital letters on." The distance between heaven and earth fades. We begin to see how deeply earth-life is grounded in its divine Source.

Each of these qualities is, in and of itself, a manifestation in creation of God's image. Prayer begins to consciously connect our "small-letter" qualities with their rich Origin and Source: "Finally, beloved, whatever is true, whatever is honorable, whatever is just, whatever is pure, whatever is pleasing, whatever is commendable, if there is any excellence and if there is anything worthy of praise, think about these things" (Phil. 4:8).

For me, at a certain point, seeing God as qualities such as the Good, the True, and the Beautiful became a channel to get beyond limited childhood ideas. One of my favorite prayer phrases derives from the old exclamation, "O my Goodness!" When some good thing captures my attention, like the sharp green taste of a fresh salad, the radiant glow of the sunset, or the simple body purr of an innocent pleasure, I am likely to attune my consciousness to its ultimate Source by inwardly whispering, "O my Goodness!" Such a prayer list of good things can continue with all the qualities that make up the rich palate of our soul's participation in the world's life: "my Strength, my Joy, my Peace, my Life."

But the divine energies influence more than the human psyche. One of my clearest revelations of the "capital letter" nature of life occurred early in the spring of my last year in seminary. Walking briskly along the campus on my way to lunch, full of high-minded theological preoccupation, I was literally turned around by the intense purple of an early-blooming iris, which caught the edge of my eyesight. In a moment's time I found my state of mind altered from busy preoccupation to calm, still, silent adoration. Flowers were not, at that time in my life, high on my list of things to pay attention to, but this flower had brought me to a halt like a burning bush. And in that moment its dazzling goodness was, to me, sheer grace—as if the color were touching my very core. I felt myself relax into a state of centered, receptive attentiveness to the radiant goodness of the moment. My senior-in-seminary intellect feebly protested, *Is it right to be worshiping a flower?* But my heart and body knew that they weren't facing some simple, small beauty; rather they were being awakened to adoration of the one and only Beauty. The flower became a doorway to the world, to grace, to God.

The unseen and unseeable God was manifest in the tangible quality of Beauty. Saint Thomas Aquinas describes this Source of all things as the *Qualitas qualitarum,* the "Quality of qualities," all-pervasive in and behind all the goodness in creation. As the fourteenth-century contemplative Julian of Norwich puts it, "God is everything which is good, and the goodness which everything has is God."[3] She is on solid biblical ground in so saying, for, as Isaiah sees, "the whole earth is full" of God's glory (see Isa. 6:3).

As our awareness of spiritual qualities grows, the words become powerful for use in extended times of meditative prayer or in daily moments of encounter with frustration. One pilgrim who crossed my path in a two-year training program had been dispirited and angered by "the use of traditional masculine images of God as a support for cultural male dominance." She found a new approach to the Mystery through claiming her own encounter with divine qualities and expressed this connection in a poetic invocation:

> Being, enliven me.
> Breath, inspire me.
> Beauty, enrapture me.
> Heart, connect me.
> Knowledge, expand me.
> Wisdom, empower me.
> Truth, justify me.
> Light, illuminate me.
> Darkness, educate me.
> Mystery, amaze me.

Grace, uplift me.
Peace, comfort me.
Center, draw me.
Oneness, embrace me.
All-in-all, use me.

Blessing, I bless you.
Love, I love you.[4]

A DOORWAY TO PERSONAL ENCOUNTER

At first glance, this attention to what seem like rather impersonal qualities may appear a detour away from the goal of a personal relationship to God. In fact, this practice can be a doorway to experiencing the love of God in and through all things.

My colleague Tilly-Jo Emerson was jolted into questioning her own expectations by someone's assertion that she didn't have a very "personal" relationship with God. She got very annoyed. Her idea of the Divine was cosmic and abstract, the Great Life of everything. She imagined that a "personal" relationship to God necessarily meant feeling as if she were with a humanlike person. This concept simply was not part of her experience.

I challenged her to consider the moments or places in which this Great Life actually touched her and moved her personally. When I put it that way, she recognized that It did: the intense red of the ornamental maple tree next to her back deck had been so vivid it seemed to call forth something from deep down inside her. She felt personally related to that Beauty. As it turned out, encounters with red maple leaves had been filled with this special, sacred feeling from her childhood; but she had never claimed that feeling as an active part of a relationship with God. "So," I pointed out, "you can claim a personal relationship to the divine Beauty and practice it. Why not do that, and see where it leads you?"

So, starting with the redness of maples, Tilly-Jo opened herself to seeing other manifestations of grace. She joined a spiritual companionship group that helped her scan actively for signs of God's presence in daily life, and she began to sense the Presence more vividly—in moments of inward spiritual support, strong images of God's protective and empowering presence in situations of her life. She soon developed an ongoing sense of personally encountering the Holy in a variety of unfolding ways.

Each one of us needs to be sensitive to the qualities that seem to be alive and compelling for us. In those qualities we will find the cutting edge of grace, God's own particular means of attracting us. I believe this attention to the living confrontation with grace is more important than an entire laundry list of "correct" beliefs. Not that fidelity to the gospel message isn't important. Simply making up our own ideas of God on a whim would be foolish. But we can be attentive to where the God described in Scripture and tradition actually touches our imagination, intellect, emotion, and life situation. For each of us, a distinct and particular pull from the Divine must be honored and followed in order for our own soul to unfold its true nature in the Spirit.[5]

WEAVING A TAPESTRY

We witness the personal quality of the divine Presence in a variety of traditional and scriptural images. For my friend, the beauty of the red maple leaves began to reveal what she called "The Allurer," the Presence that invites us to love it through loving the world. A host of familiar personal images has been used through the ages: Father or Mother, Companion or Guide, Comforter or Challenger, Warrior or Peacemaker, Friend, Shepherd of individuals or nations, King or Helper. In our journey into greater responsiveness to the grace available in the moment, we explore more than our own immediate perceptions. Our individual experiences and prejudices limit each of us. Because of that reality, the accumulated experiences of others contained in an ancient, time-tested spiritual pathway like the Christian tradition become an invaluable resource. The traditional names and images of God in Scripture and liturgy can further disclose to us the divine qualities in any circumstance.

It is crucial that we perceive all these attributes, names, and images as pointing to the various ways God works in our lives here and now rather than as static, "graven" images of a distant, remote reality. We learn more of the millennia-old witness to the experience of the Divine through reading, sharing, and listening to others tell their stories. As we learn, we can look for what leaps off the page, stirs the heart, piques our interest, or causes us to say "aha" in realization that it describes our own experience.

Over time these ideas, images, and impressions slowly weave themselves together into a distinctive tapestry in our souls, a rich pattern of ways to remember and call upon the divine Grace. Though each person's God-tapestry draws from common threads of recurrent, persistent, archetypal aspects of the Divine, we all discover a few particular aspects of God with special power to make grace available to us and to make us more available to grace.

It's important to keep adding to our storehouse of names, aspects, and images of God. We tend to stick with the familiar images such as Father, Shepherd, Comforter, Christ. But what if we're looking for the divine Comforter while the divine Challenger actually is on our case? Or we're thinking we need the Fire of the Spirit to buck up our faltering spirits when God is trying to make the Water of grace available through our own tears? What if we're looking for divine Light and illumination when what's available is the divine Darkness in a "cloud of unknowing"?[6]

A man came to me in the pain of emotional abandonment, after being suddenly dismissed from a longtime position in a close-knit family firm. Somewhat agnostic, he felt the need to reach out for spiritual sustenance. We talked about simply being receptive, asking for grace; he went off to practice the habit of sitting quietly in meditative openness, using a short breath-prayer phrase to turn his heart and mind toward the Mystery. The next year contained no great illuminations or dramatic signs. Perhaps he too had been anticipating some face-to-face encounter. What actually became available was quite different: "I finally realized that what seemed like just a quiet emptiness had a 'something more' in it, just there, just with me. I felt companioned." It was very affirming to him when I told him that this experience of "quiet emptiness" without any specific content sounded like the beginning of the imageless unknowing of traditional contemplative prayer.

Sometimes, when God seems absent or we are bewildered by God's apparent treatment of us, we are dealing with an unfamiliar face of God. All the while we feel abandoned, we may be befriended by the Unknown One who invites us to new growth, however uncomfortable or painful that may be. No single image, idea, or title can exhaust the boundless variety of divine epiphany in human life. Holding on tightly to one aspect of God constitutes idolatry. God is too deep and rich and immense to be captured in one "graven image," likeness, or name.

CLAIMING OUR OWN NAMES AND IMAGES OF GOD

Over the years special faces of the Divine have become significant to me. My own particular divine aspects may suggest additions to your collection of divine "names," to be called upon in prayer.

THE DIVINE CHALLENGER

"Challenger" or "Provocateur" was one of the first new images I added to my familiar and comfortable list. While the actual name itself does not appear in Scripture, the theme recurs constantly. "Go from your country and your kindred and your father's house to the land that I will show you," God says to Abram, setting the tone for all spiritual journeying (Gen. 12:1). The divine Love cares passionately about our fullest development and therefore constantly works through circumstances to keep us growing.

My fervent fundamentalist background had led me to believe that God was in the business of getting rid of people's problems. Personal difficulties were obstacles from the Adversary to be overcome. This construct seemed to apply to some situations, but persistent inner fears and outer difficulties simply wouldn't be vanquished so easily. Were such failures my weakness before the dark Adversary?

I began noticing in Scripture that it isn't always Satan who is the Adversary. In some of the tales, the Adversary is the Divine. "On the way, at a place where they spent the night, the LORD met [Moses] and tried to kill him," according to the enigmatic tale of the Exodus (see Exod. 4:24). Again and again, it is God who sets a "test," a great challenge or obstacle, for Abraham, Moses, the children of Israel. It is the Spirit itself that leads Jesus into the wilderness to face testing, trial, adversity, and the Adversary.

As I pondered this theme, some psychotherapy helped me discern the "shadow" or difficult side of my personality as a gold mine of spurs for growth. The scriptural image of God as Challenger joined forces with the welcoming attitude of the psychotherapist in opening a new doorway to grace for me. I began to reevaluate the so-called "problems" in my life. One day my brain quipped to me that "problems are actually probe-lems," challenges, probes, pushes, provocations to evoke new adaptation, new attitudes, the awakening of latent abilities. In a short time I went from feeling problem-ridden to probe-gifted! I perceived the psychological and situational issues in my life in a new light—as probes of grace from a divine Challenger who willed my fullest wholeness and well-being.

Such a shift in how we label something is no mere feel-good exercise. Finding ever more true and accurate names for the qualities we encounter enables finer discernment of both human and holy Spirit at work in our lives. Such corrective labeling is part of what Buddhists call "right speech," the practice of naming things as accurately as possible without a reactively negative spin. An early Christian saying attributed to Jesus calls such naming "seeing clearly what is in front of you."[7]

After this shift in my thinking, I began facing challenges and "probe"-lems with a new kind of prayer: "O Challenger, help me find what I need to use to meet you in this situation," instead of simply yelping, "Help!"

THE DIVINE WISDOM

Another long-neglected biblical image that crossed my path compellingly is Holy Wisdom, portrayed as Wise Woman and an all-pervading feminine force (see especially Proverbs 8 and Wisdom of Solomon 7–9). Wisdom is "at play" in creation (see, for instance, Prov. 8:22-31, KJV), manifesting through the innate order of creation. She also resides deep inside us as the "mother wit" that flows through our bodies and brains, underlying our capacity to adapt, survive, and create. I came from a religious background where human nature was considered devoid of grace. A whole new world opened up when I could see God's Wisdom at work in nature itself and in the sinews of my own body and mind rather than confined to a supernatural realm.

One day in prayer I felt a strong urge to take out pastels and draw. Beginning with yellow swirls on rough paper, the image of a large golden egg, shining with light, started to emerge. As I drew, I sensed that this egg represented something in me about to be born. As I finished the picture, I found myself spontaneously writing at the bottom of the page, "I am Wisdom's child." In some subtle way, I felt more at home in the universe. I only discovered later that Jesus may have referred to himself and his disciples as "wisdom's children" (see Matt. 11:19, KJV).

THE DIVINE DESTROYER

Scriptural images of God often challenge us to rethink our conventional piety. There are few, if any, Christian prayers to God the Destroyer, but Scripture clearly depicts the Lifegiver also as Destroyer.[8] This is not the wanton, twisting destructiveness of evil but the natural, life-giving process of destruction that goes hand in hand with life itself: the fire that burns away the old to make way for the new (Heb. 12:29), the dying that precedes rebirth (John 12:14), even the "thief in the night" that robs us of false securities (1 Thess. 5:2). God appears as the voice in the midst of the creating-and-destroying whirlwind of Job's vision (Job 38:1), as the one deserving blessing for both giving and taking away (Job 1:21), as "rottenness" in the house of Israel," and as a "moth" that eats the cloth (Hos. 5:12, KJV) of all that needs to pass away. These seemingly dark images of divine grace became intensely meaningful to me in a long period of losses and disillusionments. I learned to know a God vaster than life itself, working through all circumstances, even loss, defeat, and death, to bring new life.

THE DIVINE ABSENCE

Sometimes we may experience God's Presence as an Absence. Usually some familiar aspect of God has been withdrawn, and we can no longer avail ourselves of it. If we are spiritually alive, active, and growing, our relationship with God will not stay static. Classical Christian wisdom warns us that the "God" we first imagine we know will often prove inadequate in the tests of real life, just as our first impressions of father, mother, friend, or spouse are, in part, mistaken, and must be shaped by further experiences. As we live through change, our images of ourselves and of God deepen and change. The disappearance of comfort received from a particular aspect of grace can feel like loss and absence. Each image we find must be held lightly, used as a connection with living grace, not as a fetish to be clutched for security. The images that come to abide with us over time become a sort of "nest" we can return to in prayer, but real journeying will take us again and again into new and unfamiliar territory.

NONHUMAN IMAGES OF GOD

Images that reflect an aspect of the Spirit's work are not limited to human characteristics. God can be for us a soaring Eagle who carries her young (according to ancient legends) on her wings (Deut. 32:11) or solid as Rock under our feet (Ps. 62:2). We can open ourselves to the mighty rushing Wind of life (Acts 2:2), or we can find shelter from life's storms in the "cleft of the Rock," the divine Cave of protection (Exod. 33:22). The path of our growth into God can seem like climbing up a Mountain or descending into a mysterious Abyss (Ps. 95:4). God's presence may be experienced as Sunlight or Rain (Matt. 5:45). The Spirit's work in us and the world can be like the roar of a Lion or the trust of a Lamb (Rev. 5:5-6). Many of these images arise from the universal tendency to link specific characteristics with animal species and the ancient practice of depicting divine qualities with animals.

I was surprised to find the work of grace sometimes portrayed in Scripture as a serpent! Not always an evil figure, the serpent also stands for divine wisdom and healing: Moses lifts up a healing serpent in the wilderness (Num. 21:9); Christ identifies himself with that serpent (John 3:14) and calls us to be as "wise as serpents and innocent as doves" (Matt. 10:16). This serpentine wisdom moves in our very bodies and brains, keeping us alive. We can consecrate this most primeval level of our intelligence to the God of grace or allow it to coil itself around our most ornery reactivity. We can use our intelligence to create a hell of intrigue, deception, and misery for ourselves or let it take wings and bring us near to God, like the mighty serpentine seraphim closest to the radiance of the divine Light. If God wants us to grow strong and subtle in serving the good, we need to be more cunning in goodness than evil can ever imagine.

Praying the attributes of God

Whether used in times of deep meditation or called upon in brief moments, these aspects and images can draw us into the streams of divine energy flowing through the world. Through them, we invite a particular aspect of the Divine to surround and suffuse us. Learning to carry our own names for God and use them as second-breath invocations begins to stretch our sense of the many ways grace is available, especially in life's difficult moments.

Most importantly, such invocations can make us more ready to respond to the unexpected twists and turns of grace in our lives. Rather than fixating on one way we expect God to show up, we can become more sensitive to how God is actually present. We will let God be God, appearing as God wills, not as we demand. Each surprise of grace will call forth something new from deep within our own souls, shaped in that very image.

To practice using the names of God prayerfully, see Exercise 4 in the appendix. To practice discerning the qualities of grace present in situations, see Exercise 6.

CHAPTER 4

Growing into the Image of God

Sometimes a quality of human nature can become a direct portal into the Divine in the simplest and most unexpected ways. I recently led a lay pastoral-calling group in an exercise to develop a more "caring touch." The group members were looking for sensitive ways to support the dying. First we practiced reaching out and taking a person's hand in an ordinary, casual way, holding it for a half-minute. Then we practiced "deepening" the touch. People were directed to take a few moments to feel the aliveness in their own hand and to awaken a sense of intentional caring. Then, with "awakened" hearts and hands, they reached out to hold the other person's hand.

The difference made by conscious awareness and intention startled the group members. The ordinary hand-holding was "okay . . . nice . . . a little comforting." But the intentionally caring touch felt "more connected . . . tender . . . as if it was touching something inside me." One person, with tears in her eyes, said that she felt "touched by God" as her partner held her hand. We hadn't done anything very dramatic externally. Internally, however, conscious awareness and intention had opened a doorway into something more.

That experience of some human quality expanding into "something more" signifies that human beings are made in the image of God. As we saw in chapter 3, each of our deepest human potentials is based in a divine original and meant to grow up in the light of the divine model displayed most fully to us in Christ. God has fashioned us to reflect and embody the various attributes or qualities that make up the divine nature. Thus, if "God is love," we are made with the capacity to grow up fully into a mature and Godlike love. If God is justice, then our hearts will be restless until they learn to use that justice-making power. God works with us a patient teacher, using every circumstance of life to bring forth these qualities in us.

Take the attribute of divine Beauty, for instance. I'll never forget the Saturday matinee at the opera when a restless audience was brought to rapt silence by the performance of a diminutive soprano. The magic began the moment she lifted her voice in the first aria. The fidgety, coughing preholiday crowd was immediately drawn into the crystal-clear sound that filled the hall. Everything receded before this enchanting voice. I've never felt three thousand people be so absolutely still. Time stopped as we sat enraptured by something heavenly. When the singer finished the aria, utter, stunned silence reigned, followed by a long, inaudible sigh. Then waves of applause and shouted acclaim thundered through the hall. In opera, there are good performances, and then there are "moments." This was one of the moments. "Something more" had shone through this woman's offering of her whole self to the music. She had become a portal to Music itself.

It doesn't take grand opera to reveal God's image working in us. Any time we devote ourselves to an aspect of the divine nature—holding it in our minds, making the embodiment of it our aim—our Godlike qualities are called forth, grow, and become strengthened.

On two occasions a woman I'll call Martha, who has spent her life devoted to giving strong, nurturing affection, saved me from the brink of the depression I suffered from recurrently in my twenties and thirties. A biologically based condition made me vulnerable to the depression, but often it was circumstances that pushed me over the edge. One night on a church governing board retreat, and very vulnerable indeed, I found myself sitting next to Martha. As the meeting progressed, a terrible sinking feeling in the pit of my stomach intensified, and all the energy slowly drained out of me. Fortunately I was not chairing the meeting and could hide behind a socially amiable face. Yet, as I was on the verge of succumbing to despair, Martha's hand reached under the table, took mine, and held it for about five minutes, filling me with an almost imperceptible calm. Slowly my slide into the quicksand stopped, and by the next morning I was out of the danger zone.

Some years later, in another vulnerable moment, I felt an urge to get up from stewing futilely behind my desk and go out of the church into the downtown shopping district. My body literally quivered with the incoming tide of agitated depression. Out of the corner of my eye I noticed Martha a long way off but headed on a course that would cross my path in a minute or two. As we met in front of the drugstore, she smiled, told me I looked like I "needed a big hug," and proceeded to administer it. Affection flowed from her in a perceptible wave, though in outward appearance we were just greeting one another. Once again, the dark inner waters began to recede, and over the next day I found my way back to safer emotional territory.

All I know of Martha's spiritual life is that she raised a family, loved her work as a teacher of young kids, and came to church every Sunday. She had claimed her nurturing abilities and loved to care for others. I think it's a safe guess that my experience with her was not an uncommon one. Her well-honed sensitivity to other people's feelings had, at some interior level, been made available to the Source of all caring. At crucial moments, her caring became the tangible vehicle for a deeper Caring. At these times she became a portal of grace, the living image of God.

WHAT IS THE IMAGE OF GOD?

We have seen that the Bible expresses the divine image in a constellation of various qualities, energies, attributes, images, and names. The medieval Jewish mystics known as Kabbalists devised a most helpful overview of this mosaic of attributes. I stumbled on their work as I was trying to understand what it might mean to be "conformed to the image" of Christ, who is the "image of the invisible God" (see Rom. 8:29 and Col. 1:15). The Christianity I had learned seemed vague about the image of God, beyond general exhortations to be more loving.

The Kabbalists spelled out a profoundly suggestive vision of the image, which they saw as many dynamically interacting attributes: Wisdom and Understanding, Loving-kindness and Judgment, Beauty, Endurance and Majesty, "Foundation" or Creativity, and Sovereignty.[1] These last two refer to the ability to gestate ideas and carry them out, exercising rule on earth. The great characteristic of the Crown presides over all the attributes. The Crown symbolizes the Divine's governance of heaven and earth and our capacity to govern ourselves with God's help. From each divine attribute a stream of spiritual energy, formed in the heart of God, flows through human life. Human nature is built according to this model, with innate, divinely given capacities, which are designed to grow by education and discipline into cooperation with the divine attributes. Thus, the Messiah, or Christ, in this mystical Jewish expectation, will embody these attributes supremely and bring them to full flower in human nature.

In the light of this knowledge, I reread the New Testament with fresh eyes. Jesus moved in a world where early Kabbalistic ideas were beginning to take hold.[2] Jesus and the apostles use different and less tightly organized lists to describe much the same connection between the divine and human realms. Jesus seems to have made his own lists of attributes. Like his fellow rabbis, he refers to the "two inclinations" in human nature—one toward good and the other toward evil. He says that both good and evil proceed from the same heart: the person given to evil produces "adultery, avarice, wickedness, deceit, licentiousness, envy, slander, pride, folly" (Mark 7:22); the good person "out of the good treasure of the heart produces good" (Luke 6:45). Saint Paul spells out what many rabbis were defining as "good" when he says that the fruit of the Spirit of Christ dwelling in us is "love, joy, peace, patience, kindness, generosity, faithfulness, gentleness, and self-control" (Gal. 5:22-23).

I began to see more clearly that being "like Christ" involved growing up into the mature form of each characteristic. Learning to manifest these qualities in our lives takes more than just imitation, though human beings often learn through imitation of an admired, beloved model. In the slow process of growing up into Christ, we gradually become skilled in living out, in turn, various aspects of the image. Desire to emulate leads to practice of the admired behavior. Practice leads to the discovery of whatever in us may block or hinder realizing the desired behavior. So emulation inevitably leads to challenging all our immaturities.

APPRENTICES TO CHRISTHOOD

Each teaching of Christ invites us into creative conflict with ourselves, stretching us beyond stasis, stirring the latent capacities of our souls into bud, blossom, and growing fruit. Jesus' words are best taken not as demands but as challenges to disciples—to those who wish to learn from him how to mature the image of God within them.

I've become convinced that Jesus, like a good master with his apprentices, acts as a challenger, mentor, and provocateur. Each teaching of Jesus is designed to stimulate some aspect of the image of God within us. He is Master at living out the image of God, and we are called to be apprentices.

As apprentices we are, in fact, unskilled, unformed, undeveloped. The good Master will present us with tasks just beyond our reach, tasks that build on our strengths and challenge our weaknesses, and he will stand by us in our clumsiness as we learn. Our ignorance and mistakes put us into a searching, inquiring mode: How can we do this better? Are there others who could give us tips? Have we understood the instructions? Being an apprentice means starting, quite honestly, where you are rather than where you should be.

I didn't begin to take Jesus seriously as my teacher about life until the day I admitted honestly to myself that I hadn't a clue how to love my enemies. Even more than being unskilled, I wasn't sure it was a good idea.

This realization came to me in my early thirties, while struggling in psychotherapy with a big load of unrecognized emotions. I had been reared as a "good" Christian boy. I was such a good boy I tried earnestly to like everybody, no matter what I felt about them. I regarded Christlikeness as an ideal I was supposed to live up to. Maybe if I tried hard enough to live up to the Christlike ideal, the resistant parts of myself would just give up and go away.

Life wasn't working that way. Rather, I had just suppressed my real feelings in order to present an amiable facade to others and to myself. In the course of psychotherapy, I began to see the importance of owning my real feelings, especially dislike and anger.

At the same time, I agonized, *What about "Do not judge, so that you may not be judged" and "Love your enemies," or even "Love your neighbor as yourself"?* How could I obey those commands and still honor my sometimes-murderous rage against people who were doing real harm to me or to others? Finally, in exasperation, I found myself blurting out a spontaneous prayer: "Okay, Jesus. I just can't do this not-judging and enemy-loving stuff. At least not right now. What's more, I don't even know how to do it. If I'm ever going to do it, I guess I'll have to learn. And I figure it's going to take me a long time. Right now I need to practice living out my anger."

In that utterly pivotal moment in my becoming a disciple of Jesus the Life-Master, I took the first conscious step of living *into* the challenges Jesus sets for us rather than living *up to* a set of rules. I had taken the first step as an apprentice of Jesus, learning his art of cultivating the soul toward more receptivity to grace.

The image of God in us doesn't grow through pious aspirations, slavish copying of rules, well-polished public selves, or carefully guarded inner lives. We get there by the messier, slower path of learning, step-by-step and mistake-by-mistake, how to love, how to cooperate, how to forgive, how to work through harsh and dark emotions, how to trust. Part of the process of salvation, real soul-healing and transformation, lies in wrestling prayerfully with the rough places in our souls that resist Jesus' saving invitations. We need to ease ourselves into one challenge of Jesus after another. Over the years I have slowly taken Jesus' teachings, challenge by challenge, as specific practices to work with in daily life. Over time "fruit" is borne—a metaphor surely indicating the slowness of the process. As the old hymn puts it: "One step at a time, dear Savior, I cannot take anymore."[3]

ENLIGHTENING ANNOYANCES

Often we don't understand Jesus' words clearly when we begin to respond to them. I have had a slow struggle with myself over Jesus' seemingly clear challenge: "Give to everyone who asks" (see Matt. 5:42, KJV). *You can't honor every request, can you? Certainly not! What about beggars? How do you know they're for real? What if an alcoholic wants a drink? What if there are more important priorities that claim my time right now?* And yet, and yet . . . when I was in college I heard a man who simply did it. He always carried a bag of change when he walked the streets of New York; and if someone asked for money, he gave them some, along with a few moments of conversation and a warm "God bless you." He said, "The Man told me to give, not to launch an investigation. I'm not in charge of the outcome."

That testimony wormed its way into my mind, and I've never been able to worm it out again. It's been an enlightening annoyance, arising again and again to provoke me. Soon after I heard the man, I noticed how parsimoniously I served after-dinner liqueurs to my friends. In fact, a good friend said to me one night, "It's really very odd. You're so generous with some things, like your listening ear, but you're downright stingy with your Grand Marnier." To my embarrassment, I saw that she was right. So, with a reluctance that was perplexing to me, I started being less exacting in my hospitality. I even managed to marry a woman whose dinner-party style resembles that of a cornucopia, challenging me further: *Do we really have to have two entrées?*

Slowly I became more conscious of the ways my subtle stinginess compensated for my sometimes unwise professional availability. A major pattern, I came to see, is that if someone asks me to do something, I react instinctively by putting it off for a while. I'll do it in my own time, thank you. One day in meditation it became perfectly obvious that the constant "later, dear" response to my wife was a barrier to grace, another face of stinginess. I went to the computer, printed out four YES! signs in a large, elegant typeface, posted them around the house as reminders, and just started taking out the garbage when asked. Well, most of the time; I'm still practicing.

About this time my humanist brother-in-law, Keith, brought me face-to-face again with my response to beggars. He quite readily gave change to the beggar on the subway while we were headed for an outing, while I held back. I asked him why he did it. What if the man were not really a beggar? He shrugged, and said, "He might really need it. It's not for me to judge; certainly not over a measly fifty cents." The humanist was doing what Jesus said while the Christian stood aside in suburban judgment. I've now started taking extra change into the city, giving money, and surrounding each beggar with a blessing of God's light in my heart.

I'm coming to see that Jesus doesn't specify exactly what you're supposed to give when someone asks. I hear him calling me to deal in some gracious and appropriate way with the person who asks; at least to give something: "Yes, I'd love to look at this book; can it wait till summer?" "Of course, I'll get those papers for you, right now." "No, I'm not able to talk right now, but I'll call you right back when I'm finished." Give. Give something. Don't turn away. And so the meaning of Jesus' word keeps growing in my heart.

Challenge by challenge, we can let the image of God within us be provoked into a growing-up process. We may deliberately choose a challenge to work on or have one thrust at us by life circumstances. What will the next challenge be? Trying to serve God rather than mammon (Luke 16:13)? Learning to say no when we need to and yes when that response is called for (Matt. 5:37)? Speaking face-to-face, alone, with someone who has offended us (Matt. 18:15)? Taking time to go "into thy closet" to pray in secret (Matt. 6:6, KJV)? Developing a gift we've been given (Luke 8:18)? Forgiving someone from our heart (Matt. 18:35)? Reaching out beyond our own comfortable group (Matt. 5:47)? Taking up our cross—for example, being willing to speak up against oppression in a situation where we can make a difference even though it may be risky (Luke 14:27)?

The early Christian expectation is that as we grow, we will grow in our participation "in the divine nature" (2 Pet. 1:4, NIV). We are called to become nothing less than Godlike, a possibility only because we are made in the image and likeness of God. This doesn't mean each one of us gets to be a little petty all-knowing, all-powerful deity. In fact, it's a bit odd, isn't it, that when we say someone "thinks they're god," we mean that the person is behaving arrogantly and abusively! Biblically Godlikeness means reflecting the loving, just, compassionate, and discerning nature of God, not pushing people around.

More and more we become "partners of Christ" (Heb. 3:14). The qualities in our nature and the qualities in the divine nature work together synergistically, so that we literally become "coworkers" with God (2 Cor. 6:1, RCM).[4] Only in learning how to live this way do the deepest yearnings and powers of our own nature unfold in health, vigor, and grace. Nothing less than being "conformed to the image of his Son" (Rom. 8:29) and bearing "the image of the heavenly" (1 Cor. 15:49, KJV) will satisfy the deepest yearnings of the human heart. It's a lofty goal. Its full completion takes a lifetime and beyond, but it all starts with simple, everyday things like how we hold hands.

For specific steps in following the challenges of Jesus, see Exercise 8 in the appendix.

CHAPTER 5

The Altar of the Everyday

The divine likeness in us is called forth and shaped into maturity in the arena of daily life. Whether we know it or not, the spiritual quality of each encounter of the day—good, bad, or indifferent—is an offering to God. The goal is that we consciously learn to offer our "whole selves, body and soul, in a living consecration" (Rom. 12:1, RCM).

After years of trying to have a prayer life, a stubbed toe invited me to prayer. As I claimed more and more occasions of frustration and blessing, my days began settling down into an unanticipated rhythm of prayer, in which I offered up more moments into the Presence. The whole sense of the day began to change. Instead of simply having things to do, I perceived events and people, ideas and emotions as offerings to be woven into the pattern of God's love.

One day, as I was working under the gun to meet a deadline, feeling more and more burdened and boxed in, I stopped for a long, slow breath and a phrase laced through my mind: *The liturgy of the day is as important as the content of the day.* The significance of a day's spiritual quality ranks as high as any of the tasks in it. Unless heart and mind are called back again and again to ground themselves in the connected, compassionate mind of Christ, the spirit will go sour, frenzied, or reactive.

THE NATURAL LITURGY OF THE DAY

I began asking other people about times and events that inspired their own God-moments. The sense of a natural liturgy of a day emerged from these discussions—"natural" in the sense that it arises from events rather than requiring time out from ordinary activities.

EARLY MORNING

A surprising number of people, I found, consider the simple act of going down the driveway to pick up the morning newspaper an occasion for praise. "It's my way of greeting the day with gratitude," one Presbyterian woman told me. "Just walking out of the house into the big world, feeling the air against my skin, seeing the light, and getting the feel of the day awakens me to a sense of being a part of something bigger than myself." Some early risers embrace the sunrise itself, which touches a primal physical response in most everyone, as their first daily God-moment. My friend Mary Anne Bainbridge, a spiritual director, has her first cup of coffee, year-round, out on a covered porch, even sitting bundled up in midwinter, awakening to the grace unfolding in this unique, unrepeatable day. Some people start the day by lighting a votive candle on a home altar as an act of dedication and invitation.

The Jewish practice of making ordinary moments the occasion for blessing begins with the first conscious breath of the day: "Blessed are you, O living One, who opens my eyes from sleep, and my eyelids from slumber." Blessings link every action of the day to God. Some devout Orthodox and Hasidic Jews keep a bowl of water by the bedside in order to wash the hands in deliberate consecration of every "work of the hands" to God's purposes. The first formal prayers of the traditional morning devotions are so clearly connected to the actions of getting up in the morning that I've adopted them as my own and use them in relationship to those actions. The prayers take us into the bathroom, blessing God for the miracle of the body, and then through the ritual of getting dressed. My own adaptation of these ancient prayers continues:

> Blessed are you,
> who has woven my body a many-chambered mystery
> to stand and praise you.
> Blessed are you,
> who has formed me in your image to be a man [woman].
> Blessed are you,
> who brought me forth fragrant and naked in your sight.
> Blessed are you,
> who taught me how to clothe the naked.
> Blessed are you,
> who raises my body to walk the path with strength.
> Blessed are you,
> who sets the solitary in families,
> loving every tongue and tribe.
> Blessed are you,
> who makes me part of your servant people.
> Blessed are you,
> who calls me to the work of creation day by day.[1]

There are those who have learned to "pray the newspaper" as they leaf through it in their morning ritual. Instead of simply reacting with pleasure or distress to the chronicle of human folly, scandal, and achievement, they've claimed their murmurings, moans, and mutterings as prayer: "ohmigod" becomes "O, my God" as they join their inner groanings over the state of the world with the Spirit's groaning for redemption, healing, and renewal.

THE WORKDAY

Meeting and greeting with inward prayerfulness
Many people find attuning to grace easy in the morning, their sense of God enlivened by the beauty of nature or the gift of life

itself, but more difficult as they enter the busyness of the work-day. But some have found ways to bless moments at work. "I've made an act of inward blessing out of greeting my coworkers as I come in for the day," explained one office worker. "Just the acts of smiling, greeting people warmly, asking about a continuing family matter give me a chance to pray God's blessing on them in my heart." That blessing also means she's better connected to them as part of the team through the day. One personnel manager said, "My job is really like that of a symphony conductor; I've got to help people work together harmoniously. So I offer the intention to do that as I come in at the beginning of the day and hold the image in my mind of conducting an orchestra. Then when I feel I'm losing track during the day, I come back to that prayer-image."

My inquiries have turned up secret workplace intercessors. My brother-in-law David, a doctor in charge of a walk-in medical clinic, arrived one day to find the entire atmosphere full of low-grade antagonism. A usually cheerful nurse passed him with a downcast look on her face. He heard two orderlies cranking at each other. Clearly something had soured the atmosphere of this usually cooperative place. His own spiritual journey had led him to consider the practice of "rebuking dark spirits"—common to some Native American traditions as well as Christian charismatic circles. He paused briefly at the threshold, turned inwardly to his sense of God, and whispered under his breath, "All right! Enough of this!" Within a minute, somewhat to his astonished surprise, someone laughed. "In the next few minutes it was as if a dark cloud lifted," he reported. The results are not always so dramatic, but they convinced him in that moment that he could "call upon Spirit to bring healing power into a human situation."

The ability to stay centered, grounded, and open while in dialogue with a coworker can effectively inject the force for good into a work situation. Listening actively, not letting preconceptions, fears, and especially our own agenda cloud our ability to hear what another person is really saying alters the atmosphere. "This act of listening is respect for people's spirit," affirms my colleague Tilly-Jo Emerson, an organizational development consultant. "After all, when they are telling you their ideas, they are, in effect, praying to you, asking you to hear what's important to them." Coworkers may need to talk through an issue, even debate with one another, but the debate will be cleaner and clearer if people are truly listening. Tilly-Jo makes the effort, even in a secular setting, to "change business as usual to include the spiritual dimension. Good spirit flowing between people is the key to effectiveness. The inwardly prayerful person can really open the flow of spiritual exchange between people in any setting."[2]

I learned a lot about offering ordinary situations in prayer from one of the most prayerful people I've ever met: a quiet, intense, smiling rabbi named Shefa Gold, director of the Center for Devotional, Energy and Ecstatic Practice. Learning to live "in God-consciousness," or as the Jewish mystical tradition puts it, to practice *devakut*, "cleaving" to God, has been central to her life path. She has learned and teaches a variety of prayer and meditation methods, including her own form of Hasidic chant, which uses short sentences from Scripture. But behind the techniques lies the single intention we've been considering: turning toward God. Shefa's silent witness of spending up to a half hour in meditative silence in the classroom before beginning a class became a striking symbol to me of what Saint Paul means by a "living sacrifice" that leads to the "renewing of your minds" (Rom. 12:1-2). My work is teaching, and since entering a room one day that had been "prepared" to welcome students by Shefa's silent prayer, I've never been able to approach a teaching occasion in the same way. When I neglect to do the inner preparation, I can see the diminished results.[3]

Making an intention
The "living sacrifice" of the day can be to claim a single special intention, such as to be of service or to practice compassion for

everyone you meet or to follow another specific teaching of Jesus.

Shefa tells the story of a day in New York City when she chose to dedicate herself to God for the day as an instrument of serving the everyday needs of other people. She left her hotel room for a morning appointment in a nearby office building, seeking guidance about which coffee shop she might enter for breakfast, one that would give her an opportunity to be of service. Passing one restaurant, she felt a tug to enter; she went in and sat in a booth for breakfast. As she ate, she overheard a man at the counter who sounded very nervous, asking for directions. The waiter couldn't help him, so Shefa offered to help. It turned out that the man was a Jewish environmental advocate headed for a meeting with the CEO of a major corporation to lodge a protest over the company's policies. As they talked and Shefa offered encouragement, he asked if she were a rabbi. They discovered that he had heard her speak at a conference and that they had even corresponded by e-mail. Shefa gave him a blessing for his task and sent him on his way, reassured and bolstered for his witness. There was a final touch to the blessing. "As he got into a cab and I said 'God bless you' to him, a white feather floated down between us. I grabbed it and presented it to him as a token of the blessing."

While most daily intentions don't result in such an astounding coincidence, Shefa's experience is a sign of how the Spirit "in all things . . . works for the good" (Rom. 8:28, NIV), most especially when we offer ourselves in cooperation with grace. Other intentions might be to listen attentively, to welcome strangers, or to work on some aspect of a relationship.

We may need to seek guidance or clarification about a challenge we face. We can put the situation prayerfully "on the back burner" of our minds, offering our thought processes consciously to the Spirit's work, being open for anything: thoughts and feelings, images and urges, even events during the day that seem to address the issue.

One woman, separated from her husband and in a period of deep searching for direction, made her intention for the day to seek guidance about the next step. While having breakfast at the counter of a diner, a man next to her kept trying to start a conversation. She drew closer into her book, annoyed by his many questions. But as she started to leave, she turned to him and said, "I see you have something to read too." A lengthy conversation followed. It turned out that they were both separated. Then he blurted out, "You must call him if you have any doubts." As the man spoke, her inner urging received an outer nudge. They exchanged phone numbers, and she went home to make that call to her husband, which was the first step in a long but successful process of reconciliation. Ten months later while she was packing up the last boxes in her apartment the phone rang. "How are you doing?" said the stranger. "I'm moving back tomorrow!" she replied.

The point of seeking guidance is not to abandon goals and plans for the day, month, or a period in our lives. We simply need to make allowance for graceful revision. A university professor once told me that beginning the day with an extended time of conscious prayer had changed his approach to activities. "Instead of trying to make things happen, I've begun to let events arrange themselves. They do anyway, so why not give in?" He found that if he took his list of "must do, must contact, must see" into prayer and surrendered himself to the Spirit that "more often than not I just 'happened' to run into the people I needed to see just walking across campus." Of course, he still made some appointments and kept a calendar, but he found that when he phoned people they were much more likely to be at the other end of the line.

Embodying a divine quality

Closely akin to making an intention is the practice of deliberately choosing a divine quality to ponder, pray, and embody during the day. You might choose Compassion or Courage,

Faithfulness or Forgiveness, taking time at the beginning of the day to remember occasions when you actually experienced this quality. Filling the mind with these memories begins to awaken the energy of that quality in soul and body, which you may then offer to God: "I offer you my compassion that it may be graced and trained by your Compassion today." Perhaps you could incorporate a simpler breath prayer into the day: "May I be filled with your Compassion." You may call upon that Compassion while going through the day, trusting God and your own soul to bring it to mind as circumstances arise.

Embodying the qualities of God is central to our vocation as living images of God. We can learn much from others whose lives express the lively action of a particular grace. One of my early encounters with a person who truly embodied a divine quality took place in college. I'll never forget the day Lesslie Newbigin, one of the first bishops ordained in the newly united Church of South India, walked down the aisle in the choir procession of my college chapel. He literally radiated a gentle Peace, which continued to flow all through his sermon. A few years later I had a personal conference with Bishop Newbigin and perceived this same radiating atmosphere of Peace in that more intimate setting. Jewish mystical tradition would say that he had become a *merkavah* or "chariot" for an aspect of the Divine. His own soul's peace had become a carrier for God's Peace.

Carrying a person in prayer
Another workday practice is carrying a person in heart and mind in intercessory prayer. This practice does not mean thinking about the individual all the time but intending to remember and then offering the person to God whenever he or she comes to mind or in conjunction with any thought of God that arises. Medical evidence confirms that holding people in mind in a compassionate, caring, prayerful fashion can have discernible results.[4] Well before such evidence surfaced, the experience of faith through the centuries affirmed that all souls are

interconnected in God, bound together in a fellowship of mutual support and caring that transcends the barriers of space and time. Prayers holding individuals before God are not attempts to get God to do something good for those people; God is already wholly predisposed to doing good for every creature. Carrying someone in prayer involves offering our hearts and minds as channels of the Light that wants to flow through every available opening. In this act we lend part of our spirits to the work of God's Spirit in lives. Even though no dramatic or visible outcome may result from such praying, supporting people's spirits in prayer is a loving outreach whose results can never be calculated.

Discernible effects, however, do encourage us in this kind of caring. One of the most amusing stories of results from intercessory prayer comes from a woman who attended a prayer workshop I led many years ago. Being invited to "hold someone you love into the Light," this woman focused on her eldest adult daughter. As she envisioned the older daughter, the younger daughter unexpectedly stepped into the meditation and shoved the older sister aside. "You always put her first, and I'm tired of it!" she declared, much to the mother's consternation. *But, she's right,* the mother thought and focused her loving regard and God's light on her younger offspring. After the workshop, the woman went home for lunch. An hour later, the younger daughter, who lived almost two hours away, unexpectedly pulled into the driveway. Greeting her at the door, the startled mother asked her why she had made the long trip unannounced. "I don't know. Maybe you can tell me. I went out to get the newspaper and turned left when I left the convenience store parking lot rather than turning right toward home. I wondered why I had done that and then I thought, *Mother lives in this direction. I haven't seen her in a very long time, so I guess I'll just keep going.*" The mother burst into tears and told the daughter about her prayer experience, which had happened at the very time the daughter was going out for the paper. A long afternoon of discussion and reconciliation followed.

Such caring and praying doesn't right all wrongs, of course. But that kind of an investment in healing, support, or guidance for another helps make a person or situation more available to God's active presence and power.

THE EVENING

For some people, the evening simply signals a transition into more activity: office work, homework, community events; workday prayer patterns still apply. For others, evening means coming home and tending for oneself, friends or family, house, or apartment. One of the best pieces of domestic advice I ever got came from the minister who conducted premarital counseling for Suzanne and me. He encouraged us to make every evening meal special by lighting candles and holding hands for grace before meals, "even if you're only having hamburgers." The New Testament says that food is consecrated by prayer (1 Tim. 4:5, NIV). We pause, take in the savory odor of the meal, acknowledge God's goodness as its ultimate Source, and also remember the sources of our food. The most ordinary plate has links to the whole world. Its contents make plain our utter dependence on forces quite beyond our immediate personal control—the bounty of the earth, the health of the biosphere, the network of human exchanges that brings the food to our table. No wonder the rabbis teach that "the one who eats without thanksgiving is a thief"! Eating mindfully, really paying attention to the goodness of the food, savoring the presence of others if they are present, can be part of "tasting . . . that the Creator is sweet" (Ps. 34:8, RCM).

More than one person I've talked to finds dish washing a restful time for quietness, meditation, and prayer. "I actually prefer to wash the dishes sometimes rather than use the dishwasher," remarked one participant in an Everyday Spirituality workshop. "The feel of the warm water and soapsuds, the heft of the plates and pots, and the ability to look out my kitchen window to the wooded lot behind our house have all become a restful, renewing time. I have a wonderful feeling of taking care of things." Not everybody loves dish washing equally, of course, but this story serves as a perfect example of how an intention to find grace in the moment can transform a routine chore into a spiritual practice.

Having grown up in a family that considered most household chores as a never-ending drudgery, I used to inwardly resist necessary tasks like raking the leaves in the fall. Late one fall afternoon, rushing out to get those leaves raked before the light failed completely, I was more conscious than ever of how much of the task felt like a burden. Would I get it done before dark? Why were there so many more leaves this year? Why hadn't I done it sooner? Increasing awareness of the frustration and inner resistance finally sparked an "O God" response, and my mind shifted into a more prayerful space. Once more, frustration proved a doorway to grace.

It was as if the clouds cleared, and I suddenly saw that I was "taking care" not only of my property but of the earth itself. I was allowing the grass to have the space to breathe during the winter, piling up leaves to turn into rich loam for the garden. Not only that, I was taking care of my body, moving the muscles that so much wanted to exercise, keeping my body resilient and flexible. And it was an occasion to be present. The fading light of the day suddenly showed its true colors—colors I had learned to love but was blinded to by my inner turmoil—those magical blue grays of twilight. Gratitude for being alive welled up in my heart. I was no longer "cursed" to labor "by the sweat of [my] brow" (Gen. 3:19, NIV) but had been graced by an open door into Paradise, where work becomes blessed, active cooperation with God. While all my experiences of house chores have not been so pleasant since then, my attitude changed significantly. Now, more often than not, I remember that moment and can consecrate whatever task lies before me as "taking care" of something or someone, as one small part of my primary human task to "to dress . . . and to keep the earth" (Gen. 2:15, KJV).

BEDTIME

Traditionally, surrendering the events of the day into God's hands has been recognized as an important spiritual practice. The ancient service of Compline prays that the divine Love will receive our spirits for keeping through the night: "into your hands, I commend my spirit" (Ps. 31:5, BCP).

My decision to catch little bits of grace "on the run" exerted a natural pressure to offer every part of the day. I have adapted an old form of spiritual practice, the spiritual examen, or review of the day, as a bedtime ritual. For a few minutes before bed, or just after climbing under the covers, I let the events of the day bubble up into the consciously evoked presence of God as Light. I don't follow strict chronological order or try to remember absolutely everything. As moments of pleasure and goodness arise, I savor them briefly with gratitude. As difficult moments or encounters arise, they are blessed, not cursed; the rough edges are also savored but literally surrounded and pervaded by God's light. Sometimes, if an argument has occurred during the day or problems continue in a relationship, I hold the situation in the Light for a longer time. During that time my mind plays out different scenarios of how I might act or feel differently and how that might change the situation. I may suddenly see the situation from the other person's viewpoint or realize how agenda-laden my own responses were. Whatever the event, I savor it and then surrender it to the Weaver of lives.

EACH ACTION AN OFFERING

Each of our actions, each day, is an arrow sent out into the future, causing incalculable consequences. That is why the quality of every interaction carries such importance. This long-standing spiritual conviction is confirmed by the consistent report of the many people who have undergone "near-death experiences." Typically people experience a "life review" during which they are surrounded by a compassionate light and see clearly a panorama of life events. Most are surprised that little things fill the life review: a kind word to someone, being mean to a kid brother, a moment when another's feelings were hurt. They typically do not recall the great achievements or what they had thought were their major life concerns. Rather, the gracefulness or ungraciousness of encounters seems to matter most.[5] I have come to believe that consciously offering those actions daily helps bend each arrow's trajectory toward a more graceful outcome.

The offering also surrenders each event to God for God's own purposes. All our little actions are part of a larger tapestry that is being woven. We never know how today's experiences are preparing us for future possibilities or what creativity may emerge from the secret workings of God in our minds to solve an intractable problem during the silent hours of sleep.

Each person, in his or her own way, can gradually build a "Liturgy of the Day" by claiming, one after another, moments to sanctify, linking them consciously to the Spirit's presence, power, and work. This process may, in turn, lead to finding those moments during the day that are best suited for a longer period of prayer. The traditional Christian pattern dictates four times of concentrated prayer a day: morning, midday, evening, and night. Finding the place where events of the day invite even one of those traditional times can significantly enrich the occasional moments of conscious grace during the day.

But even if regular times of prayer still elude you, opening to the Spirit's presence in brief moments takes the heart, step-by-step, toward God. And sometimes one of those brief moments is sufficiently full of grace to make anyone, however importantly busy he or she may be, stop awhile and be drawn into God's presence.

To reflect on and review the day prayerfully, see Exercise 6 in the appendix.

CHAPTER 6

The Dangers of Religion

At this point a serious warning is in order: Religion can be dangerous to your health. Spiritual practices, as they grow, can actually block grace, if "turning to God" means leaving part of yourself behind. We can all too easily confuse developing a compassionate mind with thinking only "positive" thoughts while banishing the rest. When that happens, all the potent reactivity of the "first breath" of cursing is suppressed by the "second breath" of spiritual practice, rather than softened, sweetened, and redeemed by openness to grace.

The idea that we have to put our best foot forward with God has worked its way deep into many people's unconscious. But we cannot hope to please God by rejecting parts of our own soul. Such lopsided spiritual practice can do violence to the very soul God loves and created in the divine image.

Every aspect of the self, however rough, difficult, and dangerous, is meant to be redeemed and find its true place as a reflection of the image of God. Our more difficult, volatile emotions provide the primary grist for the mill of God's healing grace, full of power that needs to be turned to the good. Only as we turn all the parts of us that are not good, noble, loving, and kind toward the light will our whole self be transformed. As Jesus said, "Those who are well have no need of a physician, but those who are sick" (Matt. 9:12).

Much religion in Jesus' day and in ours shies away from this healing process, falling into the trap of piety in the worst sense of the word: keeping all the difficult stuff in our reactivity carefully out of sight by strong-willed self-control, showing a good face not only to the world but to ourselves as well. Instead of welcoming the difficult parts of the self into the light, we banish them to the darkness of unawareness, where they continue to undermine the best intentions of the conscious self.

Terminal righteousness: banishing the "bad kid"

The result of such pious suppression is what I have come to call "terminal righteousness"—trying really hard to be your ideal self and to make sure everything that contradicts that ideal self never, never gets out of hand. The history of religion so abounds with such moralism that many people think it is the heart of religion.

Jesus encountered this kind of righteousness in the legalism of those Pharisees who were determined to live exactly by the rules. One practice in that form of Judaism involved reciting passages of Scripture in order to keep "bad" thoughts from entering the mind, just as some Christian tradition encourages "bashing" unwanted thoughts and feelings until they are "dead."

A spiritual practice of idealized righteousness transcends institutional religious circles. I have worked with more than one New Age person whose starry-eyed vision of how life ought to be lived led to spiritual practices designed to shun all "negative" emotions. Rather than owning and working through difficult feelings, one young woman said that she "just let Spirit wash them away." A man struggling with serious feelings of anger and resentment dealt with them by "putting them in a box and putting the box in a closet," not just for a moment, in order to get through a situation, but permanently, to obliterate the anger. A psychology professor once told me that he'd stopped teaching meditation to his students because too many of them misused the calming phrases to avoid the reality of their emotional lives.

Jungian psychology calls the part of ourselves we try to avoid "the shadow" aspect of the psyche—all the parts in us that are the opposite of the "persona" or the ideal self we strive to be.[1] If I set my goal to love everyone, the shadow will include all those reactions in which I dislike, disdain, or hate others. We tend to want to disown the feelings that contradict our desired set of behaviors and feelings, whatever they may be. An executive who wants to reduce the workforce while executive salaries are rising, may try to let people go in brisk, businesslike fashion. Behind the hard-hearted stance, the executive may be suppressing feelings of sympathy or even guilt. Whatever is the opposite of the ideal lurks in the shadow. For people seeking to embody noble ideals, the shadow is full of ignoble impulses. For those acting ignobly, the shadow may be filled with suppressed virtues.

A noble persona does embody ideals worthy of emulation and does express real efforts to behave in public according to those values. But identifying with this outward social self may blind us to all the parts of the self that do not conform to this persona. We will seek to push out of our awareness all the "bad kid" parts of ourselves.

I witnessed a dramatic example of the "good kid" tendency of religion one Sunday morning in a church where I was guest-preaching. As I stepped into the pulpit that day and gazed down at the sea of upturned faces, I realized I was looking at a roomful of good kids, all sitting there with their best faces forward. I invited the congregation to bow their heads in prayer, and the body language as they did so visibly reflected that of obedient children.

Even as I observed them, I wasn't scorning their behavior or judging these people negatively. I was simply seeing the good kid syndrome clearly for the first time. Perhaps the effect was exaggerated in this fairly well-heeled crowd whose sense of public decorum was still very much shaped by old-fashioned, white, Anglo-Saxon, Protestant standards. At the end of the service, as I stood at the church door greeting people, I watched with growing fascination the transformation when they stepped across the threshold from the church proper into the vestibule. Not only their facial expressions but their whole body language changed in subtle but real ways. Typically the body became more relaxed, the face more animated, as each person shed some invisible constraint. Their faces became more complex, richly nuanced, and visibly more adult. I could see all the way down the aisle. Inside the church people still had the good kid face on; outside, they let it go. With a shock I understood that, consciously or unconsciously, they had to leave whole parts of themselves outside the church door! It was as if we had all been through a very sincere ritual of going inside, acknowledging that we had been bad kids during the week, telling God in body posture, face, and words that we really wanted to be good kids, and then returning to the real world with all its adult complexities and compromises, pitfalls, and pleasures.

Luther observed a similar phenomenon in the spiritual practices of his day, which insisted that a person be in a state of grace before taking Communion. Luther proclaimed a message quite different and, I think, closer to the Spirit of Christ, encouraging people to bring their sinful selves right to the altar rail. If you're not a sinner, he taught, don't bother coming, as this Supper offers the forgiveness of sins. In his Communion practice he modeled the movements of compassionate mindfulness of Christ.

When religion does not encourage consciousness of the shadow aspects of the self, the soul is split apart. The rejected, unconscious parts of the self are hated rather than loved and healed. Worse yet, what we suppress in ourselves we become highly sensitive to and disapproving of in other people. We divide the world, like the soul, into good guys and bad guys, rather than including everyone in the process of redemptive love.

RIGHTEOUS HATRED

Terminally righteous religion—whether it be Bible-thumping fundamentalism, politically correct liberalism, or idealized New

Age spirituality—is "offended" and "outraged" by the behavior of those who violate its "right thinking" rules; it scolds, intimidates, and shames, however subtly, all in the effort to produce good behavior and condemn bad behavior. The world readily divides into those who are for us or those who are against us. Those who violate our standards we can fear or dislike with impunity, never realizing that we react partly because they exhibit elements of human nature we ourselves possess but are suppressing. We may be utterly baffled by "how people can do such things," whatever they may be, clinging carefully to the cultivated sense of our own rightness. We refuse to notice the stirrings in our own nature to misbehave, break the law, behave badly, or generally cause mayhem. The intensity of these reactions stems partially from the mechanism of projection: protecting ourselves from our own tendencies to violate the norms by harboring intense feelings against those who do. Righteous indignation, contempt, scorn, and even hatred become all too easily acceptable.

A friend reported a telling incident at a church committee meeting with people fiercely dedicated to loving inclusion for all people. As the news of the call of a new minister to a local church was shared, a member of the committee wanted to know, "Do we love him or hate him?" My friend half-humorously quipped, "We're Christians; aren't we supposed to try to love even our enemies?" The group brushed aside her quip dismissively. A certain decorous hate was quite consonant with their campaign to embrace lovingly the whole diversity of the human race with the exception of people less broad-minded than themselves! In its more extreme forms, this projection of inwardly disowned characteristics onto the "other" fuels religious wars and oppressions.

SPLITTING THE SELF

Rather than bringing wholeness and healing to the psyche, such practices actually split the self, setting up some parts as worthy of love and other parts as beyond the pale. Rather than getting rid of the unwanted reactions, this process drives them into the unconscious, where they continue to operate. They leak out in sarcastic comments, unexpected outbursts, or a subtle drag and dampening of the psyche.

Jesus was deeply acquainted with these tendencies of the human heart. He saw clearly that such soul splitting produced people who "washed the outside of the cup" but left the inside dirty (see Matt. 23:25-26). The Greek word *hypocrite* signifies this phenomenon and refers to wearing a mask. Jesus rejected this religiously induced state. He said it produced souls like "whitewashed tombs"—inwardly "full of all kinds of filth" (Matt. 23:27).

Jesus thus voiced a subtle and wise insight into the suppression of emotional energy that moral and spiritual practice can produce. We see the result of such suppression when a minister who has railed vehemently against adultery is caught in the very act, when the crusader against pornography has a library full of it, or the local advocate of good manners champions the cause in a rude and assertive way. This kind of hypocrisy is not so much a conscious and deliberate deception of others as it is blindness to oneself. The ferocious attempt to identify with the good often masks a desperate attempt to control one's own behavior. The person hides behind a mask not only from others but from himself or herself.

The Aramaic word that stands behind the Greek *hypocrite* can be translated "double-hearted," an even more apt description. The good kid and the bad kid are at war in our hearts. A practice of terminal righteousness intensifies the normal ambiguities of human nature—the fact that we are often pulled in more than one direction.

Bringing the shadow self into the light

The practice of cultivating a mind full of blessing rather than cursing is the opposite of splitting the self. Instead of keeping bad thoughts, feelings, fantasies, and desires out, this practice actually *invites them in*. Compassionate mindfulness does not fear befriending the reactive aspects of the self, savoring the quality of whatever is going on, blessing rather than cursing this difficulty. Both the good kid and the bad kid parts of the self are brought into one compassionate, welcoming space.

To reject the difficult aspects of ourselves does violence not only to us but to the Creator. A long-standing Christian tradition regards evil as a deprivation of the good rather than an alien intrusion into creation. God made everything "very good." All the aspects of the image of God in us—the qualities of holiness like love and courage, faithfulness and compassion—are raw energies that need development. Like wellsprings of living water, they can flow in well-constructed or poorly constructed channels. They can be thwarted, blocked, or misused. Each of our more difficult reactions represents, at its depths, an immature expression of the image of God in us. Such reactions need to be encountered with firmness and compassion, tamed and trained to serve God's purposes. Even Satan is an archangel gone wrong.

So also, those evil things in us that Jesus identifies as coming "out of the heart" are fundamentally misshapen good things (see Matt. 15:19). The Aramaic word for evil actually carries the connotation of "unripe" or "immature," a fact that reinforces the truth of Jesus' statement for me.[2] This interpretation of evil does not lessen evil's destructive potential: immature reactions can cause enormous damage and destruction. The remedy for evil, however, is not retaliatory damning but wise restraint and persistent, redemptive love.

HEALING THE SPLIT

A spirituality of blessing stands ready to befriend any aspect of the self, become familiar with its ways, and sympathetically understand it—all the while inhibiting it from "acting out" in behavior. Jesus welcomed sinners in this spirit—as the unripe, immature, and "sick," who "have need of a physician" (Matt. 9:12). He protected the woman taken in adultery from the vengeance of the terminally double-hearted righteous, sensed the rocklike potential lurking in impulsive Peter's heart, and saw behind Nathaniel's rapierlike sarcasm an "Israelite . . . in whom is no guile" (John 1:47, KJV). The mind of Christ welcomes the unripe and immature parts of ourselves into the fellowship of the whole self, reversing the splitting of the self.

Even as we refrain from acting out in speech or behavior impulses to curse, hurt, demean, or destroy, we bless those unripe impulses rather than cursing them. We savor the quality of whatever arises in our field of consciousness, slowly discerning its energy, dynamic, and potential. Just as Jesus himself befriended the *am ha-eretz*, the rough and crude peasants of the land, so compassionate mindfulness welcomes the rough and untamed aspects of the psyche. As Jesus reached out to invite sinners to eat at his table, so we welcome our own rough and graceless ways into consciousness. As Jesus was able to stand in the presence of real evil without losing his contact with God, so we become able to see, without flinching, our deepest capacities for evil without succumbing to their power, accepting them as part of the warp and woof of the self. By seeing and accepting, we reverse the split. If we do not see and accept, the shunned parts of ourselves continue to operate by stealth and subterfuge, unconsciously.

Perhaps this process of owning the shadow is part of the mystery of Christ's "sin-bearing" for our sake: "He has borne our infirmities and carried our diseases" (Isa. 53:4; Matt. 8:17). Christ bears with us in our rough and unruly immaturity; these soul-diseases are carried into a heart of loving understanding, blessing, and healing rather than being rejected. Only in this Christlike way can the underdeveloped parts of ourselves stretch and grow toward fullness of life. Like poor misshapen plants that have been under a rock, these distorted energies come out into the light and begin to grow straight and true.

Bearing our own darkness and working gracefully with it increases our ability to bear gracefully with others whom we see acting out our own shadow elements. If we find that we must oppose someone's behavior, we will be less likely to bring a self-protective vehemence to the task. If we witness against injustice, as we must, we will be less likely to fall into a hateful warfare. Compassion for opponents—exterior or interior—leads to greater insight into their nature and creates a greater possibility of change than any holy war.

This practice of accepting our rougher responses to life's frustrations requires as much self-control as the way of suppression, but the self-control is put to better use. I don't control myself by inwardly censoring or suppressing my more difficult feelings, thoughts, or fantasies. I learn by repeated practice to allow these dark elements of myself to come out into the open to be bathed by grace. What's behind the cursing of the first breath requires careful loving attention before we can fully find the power of the second breath of blessing. Just as the patients at the pain clinic that was mentioned in chapter 1 take some time to learn how to examine the quality of their pain and simply let it be, so we may need to take some time to see clearly the nature of our reactivity.

I used to get into a cranky, aggressive mood when I had to clean up around the house. Straightening up was a bore and a chore. After much procrastinating, I would finally tackle the job with unhappy vigor. A friend once commented that the way I ran the vacuum cleaner looked like an assault on the rug. I had a pretty good idea where all that came from. My mother, a cleaning demon who prized a spotless, well-ordered house, badgered everybody in the family to keep it that way. As I child I had absorbed not only the emotional aggressiveness she brought to cleaning but my own resistance to her demand for orderly perfection. For many years, I treated this relatively minor unhappiness as an unwanted psychological inheritance to be ignored at best. I tried to feel peppy, good, and productive while I did the unwanted task. I even joked that I might as well "let Mother clean the house," since she did it so efficiently. So she did, psychologically speaking!

Then one day, as I assaulted the rug with the vacuum cleaner, I recognized a deep well of sadness in me, bringing tears to my eyes. I stopped, sat on the sofa, and took the time to let the sadness in and open my mind to whatever came along with it. Almost instantly I realized that I had picked up these feelings from my mother: a whole welter of disappointments, frustrations, and sorrows that somehow had gotten funneled into cleaning the house ferociously as a compensation. I didn't think all this through; it just came in a cascade of images and associations. I knew enough objectively about my mother's life to think my realizations were accurate. As I sat there on the sofa, virtually weeping my mother's tears, I felt a real compassion for her plight. I surrounded the image of her in my mind with my own practiced image of the light of God and spent a few minutes simply letting these difficult feelings marinate in a bath of loving grace. As I returned to the task, I continued to surround with that Light any feeling of sadness, frustration, or crankiness. Over the next few weeks and months this practice changed the way I approached the task. This may seem like a minor matter, but it led to a major healing in my life. This practice cleared the way to find my own approach to dealing with clutter, ordering my house. I began eventually to find pleasure in taking care of my surroundings rather than in "having to clean up the mess," all because I stopped trying to suppress the rough edges of my soul that the task of cleaning provoked into life.

Some of our more deep-seated and difficult reactions may call for confession, spiritual direction, or appropriate psychotherapy, which can be understood as an adjunct to spiritual formation rather than a substitute for it. With the assurance of a skilled guide, we may be less afraid to follow destructive feelings and behavior patterns back to their roots and to envision alternatives. Sometimes we cannot welcome the less acceptable parts of ourselves until someone else accepts them. The healing power of therapy or confession lies in being heard and understood by a compassionate, welcoming heart.

We are invited into just such an accepting, cleansing, healing, and correcting Love, a Love that will not break a bruised reed or quench a dimly burning wick (see Isa. 42:3). This Love sees the hidden potential in all our wild, unruly, potentially destructive reactions. It is vitally important that every "lost sheep" in the self be welcomed home, where it may find its true place as part of the image of God within us.

THE SPIRITUAL POWER OF DIFFICULTY

A spirituality of blessing does not seek too much protection from encounters that provoke the rough edges of our reactivity. Patience grows precisely in the wrestling match of patience with impatience. Without the lustful temptation to stray from commitment to a partner, fidelity does not become strong. My love for another person will remain superficial and sentimental if it ignores the rough edges and less admirable qualities of that person. We remain in relationship with friends over the long run because we have learned to bear with their foibles, forgive their trespasses, and see their less attractive qualities with compassionate understanding. Annoying and anger-making situations can become the crucible for self-control. Instead of reacting, we can practice awareness of what provokes us and consider alternative responses.

In all these ways, the difficulties of our lives are the occasions for grace and growth. All our problematic reactions can become, in a strange way, partners in our growth. This truth, once seen, becomes obvious. "I've gotten over expecting to grow spiritually without the Opposition, whether it comes from my own feelings or from outside forces," reports my good friend Nancy Orlen Weber, a gifted counselor and healer. "I just don't expect some serene, blissful, good sailing anymore. In fact, I'm beginning to look forward to what the next wrestling match will be, because I know so much growth and good will come from it."

Recognizing such potential, some Eastern Orthodox Christians see repeated encounters with the Adversary, within us and outside us, as crucial for spiritual growth. "If the Devil isn't harassing you," declare the Orthodox, "there's something wrong with your spiritual life." The Bible refers to such encounters as "the test"—our struggle with that which has the power to draw us away from God. In Scripture, God leads us into the test, making us face and deal with the reactions that arise from the depths of our souls.

It is the Spirit that leads Jesus into the wilderness, not the Devil he encounters there (see Matt. 4:1). Jesus had to face the lust for power that dwells in human nature, his own desire for magical shortcuts, his own doubts about God's providence. We might think that these temptations came from the Adversary, but the Adversary could not have tempted Jesus unless there was something in Jesus' own human nature to appeal to. Behind the simple words of Scripture we witness a real wrestling match of the soul in which Jesus finds the true sources of power: the gift of miracle instead of magic and a deeper gift of faith in God's presence and protection. Wrestling with the unripe energies of human nature, energies that could have led to evil, he finds a way to turn those energies toward the good. We are called to learn this approach to evil from the Master.

If we pray for rain, we should carry umbrellas. If we pray for patience, we should expect to find our patience tried and tested. If we pray to be more like Christ, we should expect to encounter the dark, even demonic aspects of human nature. If we want to reach the "full stature" of the humanity displayed to us in Christ, we might as well get ready to welcome, each in turn, all the immaturities that first seem to be obstacles to grace.

PART II

Offering the Obstacles

Obstacles are opportunities for grace. The dark and difficult aspects of our own nature, brought into the light of love, can actually become doorways to encountering the nearer presence of God. Each of them is, in its own way, connected with the image of God in us, though expressing itself in an immature way. If approached in a spirit of blessing, these aspects can be encountered with firmness and compassion, tamed, trained, and grown to serve God's purposes.

We are as we actually exist, rather than as we might wish to be. A spiritual practice that seeks genuine transformation of the self will neither shy away from difficulty nor seek it out needlessly but rather deal with situations as they arise and with reactions as they come.

CHAPTER 7

Holy Fear and the Wildness of God

Fear is a much-maligned friend as well as a dangerous obstacle. It can be "a fountain of life, so that one may avoid the snares of death" (Prov. 14:27). Healthy fear evokes fully awakened attention and calm poise in the presence of realities we cannot control. It cautions us before we dive into ocean breakers, safeguards us on narrow mountain paths with spectacular views, and makes us respectful when approaching the sacred mystery of any person. What little power we may have is wonderfully concentrated by fear. Fear is the mother of wisdom and the companion of courage.

This holy fear differs from being afraid, which is its near opposite: we're agitated, plunged into roiling fantasies that tug us between fight and flight. Dazed and weakened, we are disempowered. Like our first parents, Adam and Eve, we may begin hiding from life itself and God's presence in it. When the angels say, "Do not be afraid!" they warn us against this disabling state.[1]

Learning the art of life-giving fear may be the only real cure for being afraid. A friend of mine learned a dramatic lesson in the difference between the two on a wintry Vermont road. Driving with her sister, she skidded on a large patch of ice just as a car came into their lane headed right for her. "Suddenly my mind became very clear," she reported, "and time slowed down. I knew if I got scared I was a goner. I said to my sister, who gets anxious easily, 'Don't be scared. It's going to be all right. Just pray and don't say a word.' I knew I just had to stay with that mental clarity, go with what my body wanted to do, and not think about it at all. I turned and twisted, we slid from one side of the road to another and somehow ended up headed straight in the right direction on our side of the road." Was she calm? "Not exactly. It was like being really on edge but not agitated. Like, 'o my god o my god o my god o my god' all the way yet not really scared."

"On edge but not really scared"—that's healthy fear; the inner edge of awe for something other, something real that we cannot control. Healthy fear is the doorway to holy Fear, because it puts us directly in touch with life as it unfolds around us in God's world.

Holy fear is filled with *apprehension,* a great word that has taken on mostly negative associations in our century. To apprehend is a delicate, deliberate process, approaching something alert and awake to track its ways sensitively. Christ speaks of this watchfulness as an essential part of our apprehending God's presence in the midst of the powers of the world.[2]

My wife learned healthy fear of the ocean as a child.

> We knew not to fool with it because it was bigger than we were! It had its own ways, we knew; we'd been picked up by waves and slammed against the hard beach. We had to learn how to cooperate with its moods rather than trying to change it or control it. If you get caught in an undertow, you go with it rather than fighting it. You edge out of it gently. As little kids, going with this mighty flow was a thrill—to ride the undertow deliberately, zipping down the island, seeing who could go the farthest! We loved it!

In her own childlike way, she discovered that wise reverence for the awesome power of God displayed in nature can lead us to "not be timid, or play the coward" (Ecclesiasticus 34:16).

Such fear is a friend to all that is good and holy, all that invites our deepest love of life. We encounter no person or force of any importance in our lives that does not demand due exercise of fear. Fear offers the gateway into and the safeguard around the grace and joy we are meant to find in everything good. Our delight in the beauty of creation must lead us to tremble in holy fear when we realize what an assault our daily lifestyle makes upon its integrity. We cannot live as if relationships do not require serious commitments of time and energy. Scripture says that Love is as "terrible as an army with banners" (Song of Sol. 6:4). Holy fear should make us pause before neglecting or trespassing against the love relationship. Passion can be "as fierce as the grave" (Song of Sol. 8:6) precisely because it, like the ocean, has its own laws, which we violate at our peril. We cannot be heedlessly casual in Love's presence if we expect to entrust ourselves to its deep and rewarding benefits. We are not designed with power to control every potential danger that might make us afraid. We are designed to train our inborn gift of fear into an ally for living.

FEAR OF GOD?

What is true of nature and human nature is also true of the Divine itself. We need to reappropriate the importance of holy fear before the God who is the Source of creation's processes. But doesn't perfect love cast out fear? The fear to which Saint John refers "has to do with punishment" (1 John 4:18). Unless we can shed our fear of some vindictiveness in God that lurks to strike out through calamity or adversity, we may be unable to stand in holy fear before the One from whom all the mighty powers of creation flow. Absorbing the reality that nothing can separate us from the compassionate love manifested in Christ (see Rom. 8:38-39), we can face the blessings and dangers of creation with full consciousness, ready to tread with fear but fundamentally unafraid.

We can face fully the knowledge that, as gifted and as powerful as we may be, we are still small, fragile creatures who walk in the midst of titanic powers that rightly invoke breathtaking awe. The power of the storm, the intensity of sunlight, and the passionate nature of love do not aim to harm us; it is that they work forcefully, and we must tread carefully in their presence. Only as we learn to comport ourselves respectfully can we drink deeply of their goodness.

What is true of storm, sunlight, and love is also true of the God who sources all. The Love that knocks at the door of our heart is also the One who spins this world into its teeming, boisterous life. This awesome Reality has also been encountered again and again as *mysterium tremendum et fascinans*—"a tremendous and fascinating mystery."

In the story *The Wind in the Willows,* Kenneth Grahame describes a classic example of the *mysterium tremendum,* when Mole and Rat have an encounter with the divine "Piper at the Gates of Dawn."

> Suddenly the Mole felt a great Awe fall upon him, an awe that turned his muscles to water, bowed his head, and rooted his feet to the ground. It was no panic terror— indeed he felt wonderfully at peace and happy—but it was an awe that smote and held him. . . .
>
> He . . . raised his humble head; and then, in that utter clearness of the imminent dawn, . . . he looked in the very eyes of the Friend and Helper; . . . and as he looked, he lived; and still, as he lived, he wondered.
>
> "Rat!" he found breath to whisper, shaking. "Are you afraid?"
>
> "Afraid?" murmured the Rat, his eyes shining with unutterable love. "Afraid! Of *Him*? O never, never! And yet—and yet—O, Mole, I am afraid!"
>
> Then the two animals, crouching to the earth, bowed their heads and did worship.[3]

God is quite often an idea in our minds we can play with— an image or phrase we can use for our comfort or encouragement. In one sense, this is right and good, for God has allowed the divine Name to dwell among us and be taken into our hearts. But such a God is too easily our amulet, our household god, to be taken off the shelf and used at our leisure, pleasure, or need—rather than the "living One" whose ministers are "flames of fire" (Heb. 1:7), before whom the hearts of all creatures stand revealed.

"FOR INDEED OUR GOD IS A CONSUMING FIRE." —HEBREWS 12:29

My most effective baptism in life-giving fear—and the sustaining goodness to which it can direct us—was initiated by a lightning bolt cleaving through the dark thunder of a steamy night to set fire to our house.

Let me say at the outset that I do not believe that God sent the fire in any direct way. I don't think that God works that way. Modern science frees us from the superstition that lightning strikes with malice aforethought. And yet . . . and yet . . . the sense of the divine Presence in and through this event makes me feel the uncanny power of God to work through the world's wildness to bring forth good, however harsh the medium sometimes may be.

My wife and I were just going to bed as the thunderstorm reached its peak. Stripping off the last of my clothes, I stood naked in the bedroom, moved to awe by the cascade of thunder that shook the house. My heart opened to embrace the storm; I murmured, "I love this!"—and the very next moment was filled with a stunning flash of light and an odd vibrancy in the air. I felt somehow physically touched by the storm.

I heard nothing in that moment, but the neighbors say the noise was deafening, and the ground shook. I smelled the pleasant aroma of smoke and saw burning coals cascading past the window, as lovely as giant fireflies in the night. While my mind puzzled, my body knew better: it went alive, alert, calm, and calculating. I bounded up the attic stairs to behold a fire crackling in the corner. The roof was on fire.

Flashes of panic flickered at the edge of the alert focus, and I had to choose between life-giving fear and being afraid. Years of breath-prayer practice came to my aid and helped me make that choice again and again as the inner flickers of fear and outer flames of destruction grew stronger. One phone call to the fire department, one fire extinguisher, two pails of water, and a pitcher of iced tea later, we wisely decided to get out of the house.

Barely dressed, standing in the drenching rain, we watched firemen race to the attic, push over bookcases, and pull down Sheetrock to get at the fire. Fine spray surged from the giant hoses, filling the attic with mist and steam.

The war between panic and awestruck fear continued. One level of my mind wrung its hands in panicky dread: *Oh my God, we're going to lose everything . . . this is a catastrophe . . . what if it burns down? No, no, it can't, it just can't. All my books, all my papers, all the pictures, all the memories.* But a deeper level simply stood in sober apprehension, taking in the scene: *This is real. . . . This is actually happening. . . . This is what happens to people in life.*

An inner moment of decision arrived as flames visibly broke through the roof and flared up into the night. I had to face the awe-full possibility the house might actually burn down. I had to choose between facing reality and being afraid. I do not know how the grace to do it came, but in that moment I was able to surrender the whole situation into the hands of God, come what might. *All right,* I thought, *if we lose it all, we lose it all. We shall be then, as we are now, in the hands of the living God.*

This was not precisely a comforting thought. Soaked to the skin, I felt naked and vulnerable in the dark night. And yet at that moment, and somehow because of that vulnerability, I received a strong inner assurance. I knew that all this was somehow to be used for purification, strengthening, and renewal.

The house did not burn down, and what might have been great loss turned simply into major inconvenience—and great, though costly, blessing. Dealing with a partly destroyed roof and an entire interior savaged by water, my wife and I discovered inner muscles we didn't know we had as we wrestled insurance, the mess, repair and renovation, all the while running a business and carrying on a ministry. I felt harrowed by the ordeal of it all, minor though it may have been—harrowed and thus opened to the fragile beauty and goodness of life, as if the fire had burned some protective layer of innocence off me that acted like a buffer between me and the rough edge of life. Subtly changed, I became more decisive in leadership and more forceful in teaching.

In a real sense we will never feel innocently safe in our house again. I don't quite want to. I had never received in my own flesh the knowledge of how fragile the security of a house is—and how precious the simple gift of shelter. Standing in the wreckage of the attic the day after that 1994 fire, I found myself realizing that the citizens of Sarajevo were going through much worse that very minute, and now I had the barest taste of what it must be like for them. I found a quicker compassion for disaster victims of all kinds. Having lost so little, I can only stand in admiration of the fortitude shown by those who "lose it all."

Certainly we do not take thunderstorms for granted—ever. Not that we cower afraid before them, though it took a while before either of us could get through lightning and heavy thunder without tears coming to our eyes. Those natural phenomena simply make us aware of our smallness in the scheme of things. Life quivers in its very aliveness.

I learned on a deeper level than ever before that both creation and creation's God are wild. I cannot shake the conviction that I was touched by God through that lightning bolt. God may not have directly caused the fire but was somehow fully present, ready to work through those events to foster the changes that came. The divine glance shines through even disaster to touch and transform, saying, "Be not afraid," even as we stand in holy fear.

The wildness of God

It's a wild world, and surely the God who dances in its torrents and tides is a wild God. A due sense of holy fear in the face of this wildness can fuel both awestruck adoration and an urgent desire to meet the challenge of life in this kind of universe.

Wildness is not necessarily arbitrary or whimsical. It has patterns all of its own, which can be discovered by watchful observation and careful approach. We call creatures "wild" when their ways are not our ways (see Isa. 55:8) but their own deep life patterns. The weather is wild in this sense, as is the ferocious Love that works through all means, including life's dark storms, to mold and shape us into full-fledged partners of the divine dance.

Job discovers, in his great vision of the One who dwells at the center of the whirlwind, that the Divine is not safe but very good. The ways of a God who works through the wildness shatter Job's naive belief that righteous behavior provides immunity from the raging storm. Job had heard "by the hearing of the ear" of various sorts of lesser gods—a god who hurls the lightning of reward and punishment, a god of safe comfort—but now he sees face-to-face the divine Presence that dances in a universe of titanic forces.

> Is the wild ox willing to serve you?
> Will it spend the night at your crib?
>
> . . . .
> Can you put a rope in [Leviathan's] nose, . . .
> Will it speak soft words to you?
> Will it make a covenant with you
>   to be taken as your servant forever?
> Will you play with it as with a bird,
>   or will you put it on leash for your girls?
>
> —Job 39:9; 41:2-5

The wild ox and Leviathan here stand for all of creation. If you want to love me, God says, learn how to love the Real Life I give, here among these titanic forces. God invites the Job in us to open eyes wide enough to see the way God's world really is and then "brace" ourselves (see Job 40:7, NIV) to live in it, with all its fearful and wonderful powers.

Holy fear can waken us to that uncontrollable Immensity who works for good through all of life, dancing even in the midst of danger and destruction, whispering, "Do not be afraid!" Perhaps only then can we approach life with the full reverence it deserves, fearful only that we will miss its unspeakable glory or fail to apprehend the awesome Friend who dwells even at the heart of the whirlwind.

CHAPTER 8

Wrestling with Wrath

A nger is both blessing and curse. As blessing, it is part of our survival equipment, mobilizing us to fight when we must. Anger can mobilize us to confront the bully, defend what is precious, and refuse to make peace with oppression. But it easily becomes a curse—a twisting, seducing excitement that can diminish our capacity for grace. Good for arousing us, it makes a dangerous counselor and an inept strategist for actually increasing good in the world. As Scripture wisely says, "Your anger does not produce God's righteousness" (James 1:20). Anger's arousing call must be followed by something other than more anger for grace to flow.

I'll never forget the first time I was so angry I wanted to kill someone. A friend of mine in seminary, whom I'll call Joel, had betrayed me grievously, at least in my own mind. I had no idea how much anger I felt, however, until one night when Joel and I were watching a TV comedy with some mock combat. After the program, we started a mock fight, just kidding. Without warning, rage welled up within me, and the fight became serious for me. I chased Joel down the seminary campus to his second floor room, where he, still playing, crouched on the windowsill. As I stood there, panting from the run, I knew part of me wanted to push him out the window. At the same moment, I realized another part of me wouldn't do it for many reasons: fair play, moral duty, simple mercy for the vulnerable, and continuing love for a friend, however problematic he might be. In God's good grace, the better part of me restrained my vengeful wrath.

Such wrath is as old as the story of Cain and Abel in Genesis. This tale of one brother's anger against the other is the opening scene in the Bible's stark portrayal of postparadisiacal life, the introduction to humanity's bloodstained history. We can feel Cain's presence in us whenever anger, envy, and rage inflame our souls and bodies. What power can tame that conflagration?

Part of the answer to this question comes in God's response to Cain's brutal act. Despite the intense divine aversion to the first murder, God does not strike the sinner down but rather desires to "remember mercy," even in times of wrath (see Hab. 3:2, KJV, RSV). God seeks not to retaliate but to stop, at its outset, the betrayal and bloodshed that come so easily and often in the human story. Divine wrath does not strike down Cain.

The divine behavior sets an example here for us, who so often feel the murderous rage Cain experienced, whether in response to personal betrayals or in reaction to the evils of the world. Instead of punishing, God seeks to bring the murderer into *awareness* of the heinousness of the crime, to *remind* him of his kinship with the victim, to issue a challenge to master the "crouching demon" of sin at the door, and to offer *protection from vengeance* (though the "mark of Cain" is often misunderstood as a curse).[1] (See Genesis 4:1-6.)

Scripture shows us again and again a God who cares enough about the betrayal of life's goodness to react with anger. Among the rich variety of expressions for anger found in the Hebrew Bible are these: showing an angry face, smoking, snorting, raging, fierce heat, furious heat, trembling, angry sadness, fierceness.[2] Yet this God "seeks to be conquered" by mercy, rather than react in wrath.[3]

This image of a God who demonstrates how the heart can move from wrath to mercy is central to the scriptural saga. Too often in our attempts to flee from primitive ideas of a vindictive

God, we seek to banish the tales of divine wrath. But many of these stories can teach us a process by which we can break the cycle of frustration, anger, attack, and counterattack. While not true of every "wrath story" in the Bible (one thinks of the blood-thirsty rhetoric of Nahum and the relentless wrath of the Revelation), the theme of mercy's triumph over wrath consistently recurs from the Garden through the Flood and the Exodus and on through the prophets to Jesus' own teaching.

How else can the Cain in us keep from killing Abel other than by remembering that the object of our wrath is also our kin, just as I remembered that Joel was my friend? This kinship-love—*chesed*, "merciful kindness," fellow feeling, compassionate connection—is the chief characteristic of God, whose wrath guards the goodness of nature and human nature as a mother bear guards her cubs. Thus the storytellers set out here in Genesis a theme that, in the New Testament, will find its fullest expression in Jesus' challenge to "love your enemies, do good to those who hate you, bless those who curse you, pray for those who abuse you . . . and you will be children of the Most High; for he is kind to the ungrateful and the wicked" (Luke 6:27-28, 35).

THE STRUGGLE BETWEEN AFFECTION AND ACCOUNTABILITY

Surely any parent understands the wrestling match of wrath with merciful kindness. As the young father of a teething infant quipped to me wryly: "They drive you totally up the wall, and just as you really want to kill them, the little buggers seem so cute and helpless it just cuts through the anger." We seem to possess an inborn balancing capacity to check our violence against people we love. It's only a tendency; tragically some people seem to lack it. We must cultivate the inclination toward a healthy balance. Considering how easily our anger is aroused, "the real surprise is not that there is child abuse," says that young father, "it's that there isn't more of it!"

This balancing of wrath and a love that can be merciful runs through all our relationships, beginning with parent and infant.

In later years, children are likely to arouse our wrath by going against the grain of what is good for their well-being and healthy development. The father of the teething infant did a good job himself at provoking such wrath in his teen years. My wife and I took him in after he had defeated his family's ability to deal with him. Too clever by half, he often used his highly infectious charm to wiggle shamelessly out of trouble. One weekend he'd planned a camping trip for our church youth group and raised everybody's expectations with the prospect of a quiet meditation during the beautiful sunset on the lake. Busy in the office, I'd sent him out to the parking lot to meet the other kids and get the cars packed so we could get to the campsite before dark. But when the time to go arrived, he was standing surrounded by unpacked boxes of food and sleeping bags, charming a bevy of girls. I was angry and showed it. By the time we loaded up and headed out, we were too late to get ahead of rush hour traffic. The meditation he had planned was already a lost cause—to say nothing of the hassle we would face by arriving in the dark.

We drove along in silence while I fumed, listening in my overheated head to various lectures that might make him feel guilty. Surely he had to learn his lesson! Finally he coughed, turned on his dazzling smile, shook his mantle of black hair out of his eyes, looked at me soulfully, and asked, "Do you forgive me?" As my righteous desire to scold, my real concern for his moral education, and my deep affection warred within me, I knew I dared not be seduced into simply saying it was all okay. I also knew that, for his sake, I dared not take the path of blaming and imposing guilt. A typical parental dilemma. "Of course I forgive you," I finally said. "So you can turn the charm off. You don't have to try to win my love back right now because you haven't lost it. We're not talking about forgiveness but consequences. You had a job to do and you didn't do it; you blew something valuable for yourself and the other kids. You've got to face that and do something about it if you can." More silence. Finally he responded, "Well, couldn't we meditate by the campfire?"

He'd taken a step toward responsibility. I'd learned a lesson in balancing wrath and mercy. We'd both tested and strengthened our love.

WRATH AND MERCY: THE DIVINE MODEL

Just so, all the tales of God's wrestling match with wrath spell out the steps of a strong, tough love that faces what is wrong without softness while embracing sinners with compassion. What happens when the First Parents break the boundaries and stumble greedily into a terribly awakened consciousness that makes them tremble with fear and shame? We may be so accustomed to cringing through what may seem the divine tirade against the man and the woman and the serpent that we miss the astonishing, merciful ending: "God sewed garments of skin . . . and clothed them," delivered them, and gave them strength (see Gen. 3:21, KJV; Wisdom of Solomon 10:1-2).

Often we find it difficult to see the bounteous mercy in these ancient tales because we've determined the tone of voice in advance. We're sure that God, especially that alleged Old Testament God of wrath, is yelling at Adam and Eve.[4] But there are no stage directions; no notes say, "loudly, with contempt" or "coldly, with menace." It might just as well be "hotly, with frustrated love" or "tearfully, with fearful concern." We need to interpret these stories as God's wrestling matches with wrath, in which mercy constantly triumphs, and follow the divine example in our own frustrated reaction to life's injustices and evils.

When Abraham argues with God about the judgment of the sinful cities of Sodom and Gomorrah, for example, the story is not about using clever bargaining to cool down a primitive, vengeful deity bristling with rage. The language is that of the law court, not the bazaar. God teaches Abraham how to weigh opposition to the destructiveness of sin and loving hope for redemption.[5] God models how a merciful judge must investigate firsthand any allegation of "grave sin," treat people as innocent until proven guilty, and be predisposed toward loving-kindness.[6]

Abraham is not persuading God to relent but discovering that the merciful Judge will save the city if at all possible. If only ten can be found to be the "saving remnant" from whom rehabilitation can grow, there is a chance! (See Gen. 18:16-31.) Alas, not even ten can be found. The mob seeks to brutalize the very messengers who could have saved them from doom.

Whenever divine Wrath appears, we are meant to follow through the sequence of changing emotions to the very end, instead of running away scared from the fierce heat at the beginning. Usually we see God wrestling through the dark clouds of wrath to find the sunshine of mercy, to hold the sinner accountable but find a way of redemption. The prophet Hosea, in one of the Bible's greatest passages, hears the divine Love emerge triumphant from its agonizing sense of betrayal by Israel's sin:

> How can I give you up, Ephraim?
>   How can I hand you over, O Israel? . . .
> My heart recoils within me;
>   my compassion grows warm and tender.
> I will not execute my fierce anger;
>   I will not again destroy Ephraim;
> for I am God and no mortal,
>   the Holy One in your midst,
>   and I will not come in wrath.
>   —Hosea 11:8-9

WRATH AND THE DIVINE IMAGE IN US

We might prefer a less passionate, less down-in-the-mud-with-us picture of God. But this image shows us what it means to live out the divine image planted within us. We too are meant to struggle through our feelings of righteous or unrighteous wrath until we find the thread of mercy and follow it to a creative, redemptive response in the end.

Wrath is not some mistake of human nature. Wrath arises because something *matters to us*. Indeed it is the flip side of love:

someone is violating a value for which we care deeply. A leader at work behaves abusively; a corporation pollutes the river that runs through the neighborhood; someone we've trusted betrays us; no one will step forward to help with a worthy cause. For such circumstances to provoke our wrath is normal and natural.

I'll never forget the advice of a wise pastoral counselor when I responded in seething anger to a difficult parishioner. I expected the counselor to help me get over my anger, but he stunned me by saying, "You're right to be angry. This person is very ill emotionally, and the anger you describe is the response of your health to that sickness. You hate it, and hate it rightly, because it is destroying the person and infecting the group. You need to take that anger seriously as a symptom of how wrong this all is, then do all you can to deal lovingly and justly with the situation. Don't let the anger master you; use it to help keep you clear about the sickness at work here."

We cannot banish wrath, whatever its guise—from annoyance to hate; we can only accept it, work with it, learn from it, work through it, redeem it.

THE ONLY ANTIDOTE

When Jesus challenges us to love our enemies, he speaks from a rich tradition of seeking to find and follow the path of *chesed* through a world filled with brutality, betrayal, and vindictiveness. With supreme practicality for such a world, he offers us the only antidote, the only way to resist the demeaning and discounting that demonize others into "bastards," "monsters," or "beasts" worthy of our murderous rage. It is the strategy Gandhi chose to lead India to freedom and Martin Luther King Jr. adapted to fight American racism; it is the secret Nelson Mandela found in prison and the path Archbishop Desmond Tutu and countless other South African Christians used to gain a black victory in South Africa without retaliation. Some women and men through the ages have followed this way long before its modern formulation as the political strategy of nonviolence.

It is the all-encompassing compassion that seeks redemption for both victim and victimizer.

My own most intense learning about wrestling with wrath came in relationship to my own father, a highly responsible man afflicted by high anxiety; a violent temper; and a critical, demeaning tongue. Not knowing how to express his love directly, he redirected love into hard work, financial provision, and verbal demands and harangues, which left deep scars in both his children. When my mother died, I had to face dealing with this man, now old and sick, in a more direct way. I realized with some horror that I really didn't want to have anything to do with him. My own resentment and quiet wrath were too deep. Fortunately for both of us, there are commandments: "Honor thy father and mother. . . ." "Forgive others their trespasses. . . ." "Love your enemies." I knew enough to know that these commandments wisely point to the wellsprings of life. I knew I had deep heart-work to do.

I had long since gotten in touch with my wrath and acknowledged there were valid reasons for it. Now I had to search for mercy. One day it occurred to me that if I couldn't love this man as a father, I could at least treat him the way I might treat a difficult parishioner. This reframing defused the emotion enough for me to start calling him regularly to talk, listening to his life with a pastoral sympathy and treating his unpredictable outbursts of irascibility with as much clinical objectivity as I could muster.

Slowly my feelings began to change. I started imagining a small—very small—aperture in my heart-space where I could focus just a narrow beam of light on him—a cautious version of my intercessory prayer practice of bathing people in God's light. Professional sympathy began to grow into moments of real empathy. And over time I began to see him more clearly. Some of his behavior had been inexcusable, destructive, wrong. But inexcusable deeds do not mean an unforgivable person. I began to have flashes of insight about the fear and pain out of which some of these deeds had come.

Beneath my own wrath, I slowly discovered a mightily frustrated love. Like any little boy, I had wanted to love my father; that blocked love was still there. Gradually, over a period of years, merciful kindness began to dawn. I began to see the heroic battle my dad had actually fought to keep his temper and violence under restraint.

One evening on retreat, the leader challenged us to pray for a dream about someone we hadn't forgiven. That night I had an intense dream about my father as a young man. He was palpably real, three-dimensional, vividly present—full of eager longing for love, acceptance, a chance to do a good job at living—experiences his life had not really given him. When I awoke, I *knew* him—and mercy triumphed over wrath.

Just so, God knows us, heart to heart. And God knows that the only way Cain will learn how to stop killing Abel is by feeling after and finding Abel again and again in his heart, no matter how strong the winds of wrath may blow.

CHAPTER 9

Ordinary Resurrections

Dealing with Depression

 Sometimes you have to go through hell to get to heaven. My first major depression seemed like the devil itself, dragging me down to the pit—flesh cold, heart dead as stone, mind empty as night. Antidepressants, grit, and loving support dragged me slowly from its jaws. I was sure I had been delivered once and for all from the bowels of hell and knew enough to maintain my stability on the bright surface of life.

The second depression, two years later, was a crushing blow. It was an enemy to be fought against with every bit of determination I had. When the third came, a year later, I began to realize that I was wrestling with a stranger problem than I had thought. In fact, what I had at first taken to be a dark, demonic visitor was beginning to reveal itself as a teacher, albeit unwelcome. I began to consider that the dark visitor with whom I wrestled might just be a messenger, however hidden its name, face, or intent. I began to pray that it would bless me, as Jacob's dark angel had blessed him. (See Gen. 32:22-30.)

The blessing, slowly disclosed, was a deeper understanding of the nature of resurrection. I discovered that the repeated "descent to Hades" taught me the simplest form of resurrection, the power simply to get up, to stand up in the darkness, however weakly, and to move forward. Life knocks you down. You get up, raised by your willpower alone but aided by forces more subtle than you can ever calculate. As I wrote in my journal:

> Your Life, O Christ, is the power to stand,
> rooted in compassionate courage
> in the midst of and after the blow of any dark power,
> for you, O Lord, compassionately endure all things.[1]

Resurrection does not wait for Easter's exultant dawn, for resurrection begins in predawn chill and gives us the way to face every cold season or dark night.

An important initiation into learning from the unwelcome visitor came in the depths of the first, suicidal depression. People didn't know, so many years ago, that my form of depression was more physiological than psychological, rooted in the biochemistry of my body, so the therapist and I frantically sought the emotional reasons for it. In one of my blackest moments, my wife asked me, "What do you want out of life?" Agonizingly I gave her a very high-flying, pious response: "I want to grow to my full stature in Christ—and just look at what a wreck I am." Her eyes twinkled, and her mouth turned up in a familiar sardonic grin. "Maybe you should set your aims a little lower for the moment." By some odd quirk of grace, her comment struck me as funny; and we both burst into uproarious laughter, a moment of bright sunshine in a bleak landscape. The bleakness returned quickly, but I began to aim my expectations a bit lower—a task made easier by the fact that severe depression can generate gratitude for the smallest crumb of kindness, good feeling, encounter with beauty, or ability to complete the simplest task. I started to recognize that grateful acceptance of the slightest "lift" as the way back to life from the land of the shadow of death.

I had always been a person of high expectations, seeking a life full of joy, excitement, ideas, thrill, energy, and accomplishment. Now I readjusted my expectations. I began to appreciate the ordinary forms of resurrection—like the ability to get out of bed in the morning.

ORDINARY RESURRECTION

Resurrection is a simple word to describe a process so ordinary and recurrent that we may not connect it to the great expectations of deliverance the Holy Words inspire. The Greek for resurrection gives the clue to this ordinariness: *anastasis* means simply "standing up." We all lie down. We all rise up. Every day. The same word is used for Christ's resurrection. Christ reveals it as the secret of his way through life: *ego eimi anastasis kai zoe,* "I am resurrection and life." Resurrection-life.[2] Getting up again, no matter what lays us flat. If we embark on our understanding of resurrection at this simple point, the very fabric of ordinary existence can come to seem the resurrection of the dead itself.

Do I wake myself up in the morning? No. I am awakened by an innate power in the mysterious body, if not by sunlight or sound of a loved one's bustle. Letting the miracle grasp us begins here, with the mystery of any awakening. As the synagogue prays every morning, "Praised are You, Lord, who restores the soul to the lifeless, exhausted body."[3]

We begin learning ordinary resurrection in infancy. What compels an infant to crawl, to stand, to fall, to wail, and then with joyful smile to stand again and brave the challenge of the path? The muscles and the mind begin to learn the lesson of standing again, facing the terrors of the path again and again.

No, Resurrection does not wait till Easter morning. It is the life power the seeds and bulbs yearn for in the cold night of Advent. It is the light that delivers us, not so much by rejecting the darkness but by entering the darkness with compassionate bravery, looking for what is lost there.

Although my depressions were essentially physical in nature, I did discover a psychological layer lost in that darkness—a deep pool of bitterness. Bitterness over the depressions themselves, bitterness at my body for being flawed, bitterness at God for having made me and the world this way. I could understand some of the bitterness; but it was deeper, more resentful, sharper than

I could account for, like the "bitter waters" the children of Israel encountered soon after their miracle of deliverance.

Fundamental to my resurrection-learning was a motto that occurred to me one day: "There's no situation so bad that with a little effort we cannot make it a lot worse!" This motto, born in bitterness or rather in the acceptance of bitterness as a fact, evolved into a major component in curing the bitterness.

What do you do when the light goes out? Tilden Edwards suggests a meditation form that carried me through many dark episodes. Imagine that you are in a dark cell with a small portal of light above you. You honestly acknowledge being in the "shadow of death," but you keep affirming that opening to the light and availing yourself of its promise.[4] Over time such a meditation affects the chemistry of the body, connecting the portals of the embodied soul to the "goodness of the LORD in the land of the living" (Ps. 27:13).

We cannot make the bitterness go away. But we can put the Goodness into those bitter waters, and they slowly become transformed. The goodness of praise, the goodness of gratitude, the goodness of relationship are placed right in the midst of the sorrow, the bitterness. The dark feelings are not denied, but we call something else into their midst, as Moses throws the stick into the bitter desert pool to make it drinkable for the children of Israel, whose only tactic for coping with suffering had been unremitting complaint. And then, from the very depths of the waters themselves a change begins, as it can begin in our hearts. The waters are sweetened and made drinkable.[5]

I received a powerful aid to this sweetening on the Good Friday morning when I read the great psalm of Christ's agony on the Cross. At the line "Yet thou art He that took me from my mother's womb and lay me upon my mother's breast" (Ps. 22:9, 1928 BCP), I was stunned to realize that this pain-wracked person was bringing to mind the comfort and consolation of his mother's love rather than letting himself be engulfed by his pain.

Deliverance may not be external, of course. It was not so for

Christ on Good Friday, nor for millions of souls since. But even in the worst circumstances, the waters of the soul may be sweetened to new life by surrounding the horror with remembrance of goodness and the reality of compassionate love. And who can ever predict what further resurrections may come from entrusting ourselves to such love?

CHRIST'S RESURRECTION-POWER

After this realization, I began to read the Christ-story differently—not as a saga of defeat followed by triumph but as a triumphant journey through all the seasons of the soul. Advent. Incarnation. Atonement. Resurrection. Sometimes the very words, locked into stained-glass categories, obscure the truth. They lead us to scan the far horizon for bright rays of deliverance, while its simple power pulses near at hand. We think that the seasons of the church year merely trace the life of Christ sequentially; when in fact, each season, in turn, manifests a different aspect of one holy, loving Power at work in our lives. Each in its own way speaks of Resurrection.

This reading is in fact one of the most ancient ways of understanding the Christ story: that Christ's whole life "brought life and immortality to light" (2 Tim. 1:9-10) for all those dwelling in "darkness and in the shadow of death" (Luke 1:79).[6] Though we dwell in God's own creation, our weakened sight cannot see it as it truly is. Though we are sustained by God's goodness every day, our minds are so full of fears and cravings for superficial stimulation, we hardly notice the miracle of daily bread. Deadened in body and soul, we struggle to trust the compassionate connection that creates a pathway to cooperative living. The Light incarnate at Christmas begins to pervade this shadow land in every step Jesus takes, victoriously seeping into the chaos of our insanity to take the imprisoned image of God within us by the hand and help it stand again, sane and whole.

Deliverance begins not by rescue but by arousal from the deadening, daily, sleepy stupor of sin, all that separates us from

God's life in us. Befriended in our fear, hardened hearts are touched by God's goodness, however dimly perceived, and aroused to possibilities still undreamed.

The descent of the Living Word to dwell among us, "full of grace and truth" (John 1:14), shows us a different way to approach both the blossoming joys and the inevitable sufferings of this life. That way is not anchored in pain but in the goodness of God's very presence in the midst of all life's circumstances.

Seeing Christ's resurrection in this broader sense allowed me to invite Christ into the dark places of my depression. As I wrote in another journal entry:

> Feeling Your Way deeper and deeper
> through every Dark Realm
> You came to the Bottomless Pit of Fear
> and closed it round with the embrace
> of Your compassionate gaze,
> comprehending it within the wider Assurance
> that everything can fall, finally,
> only toward Your Life.

Christ does not suffer in order to triumph. Rather, his way of dealing with suffering is already a victory. Christ's way of suffering differs radically from our ordinary approach. We have come to believe that suffering in and of itself is good for us, even redemptive—a kind of "no pain, no gain" spirituality. This attitude often stems from an underlying fear that we deserve to suffer.

The whole biblical story of Christ is meant to deliver us from this hellish state of mind. Deliverance does not come when pain ends but can arise in the ordeal of it. Christ's way of entering our suffering is resurrection-life, *Zoe*—eternal life, not after death but "life-now-eternally-springing." This life is always available to any awakening trust in God's goodness: "All [things] that came to be were alive with this Life [*zoe*]" (John 1:3-4, RCM).[7]

Such life does not lie far out of our reach, high and exalted. The stuff of which our everyday lives are actually made holds this eternal life, if we have the eyes to see. My journal carries the record of this realization in a prayer:

> You laid bare for all to see how they lurk at the heart of
>   every situation,
> seeds of goodness hidden in the hardest, darkest shells
> waiting to be unlocked and stand up again.
> Overwhelmed by the tidal waves of Your world
> we yearn for Your rescue, pining for some other kind of
>   Presence
> than the still, small pulse of life within us.

THE STILL, SMALL PULSE

One day in Israel, I encountered a vivid picture of the resurrection-power I was learning to trust. After passing scene after scene of brutality, horror, and fear in Yad Vashem, the memorial museum of the Holocaust in Jerusalem, one comes to a stunning photograph of a Jewish freedom fighter captured by the Nazis. She stands, tall and straight, flanked by a cowering colleague on her right and a casually brutal S.S. officer with a gun to her left. Her arms extended at her sides, the palms of her hands facing forward, she stands in an elegant gesture of surrender—or is it prayer? Her chin is raised, her eyes closed, her mouth firm and just barely smiling with the hint of some secret triumph. Captured, she is not defeated. Her colleague succumbs in fear to the terror. The Nazi is possessed by his inner darkness. She alone is free, however bound. In her Resurrection shines. I sat down right there with my journal to capture this vision in words:

> This is how deliverance begins
>   in our world of death dealing
> and social unraveling, in places where
>   the mean and ugly triumph
> or the mind is pulled loose from its moorings.
> You do not curse the darkness but face it directly.

> You do not blast evil with contemptuous righteousness
> but shed the light of your powerful presence
>> in its very midst.
> You do not shine to expose its ugliness
> but to reach deeper into the soul of every demon
> to find the lost, hurt, distorted Image of God there.

I dare to hope that the calloused soldier could not get the Jewish patriot out of his mind, that she troubled him into salvation by awakening the dormant humanity within him. We are saved less by reformation than by reconciliation with goodness. The severed part of us that stands in rebellion against our good, against others, and against God needs not just restraint but restoration. That separated part joins the whole only by dialogue with the rest of the self, with the other selves around it, and with the Spirit that moves through all.

This need for dialogue is as true for the severed parts of a society as it is true for the fragmented parts of our inner self or the warring parties of a church. Christ does not beat up the darkness or those in darkness. Rather his light caresses them back into robust life.

The Victorious Christ has made the journey all the way to the pit of hell, to the most severed place, to the center of the tormented soul and opens it to the supreme light. We may not take the path he presents, but it lies before us. We are invited to walk in the way of resurrection as we approach the difficulties of a world where evil seems too often to spoil the good and batter the soul. "Human wrath does not work the justice of God" (James 1:20, RCM). In Christ, our very human nature itself received the power to stand up again, tall and straight, from deepest hell to highest heaven, and the passage between all the parts of the world opened again. This standing up is nothing more or less than the compassionate courage that allows us to go on in the face of anything.

THE PATIENCE OF RESURRECTION

Of course, we are still called to grow up into "maturity, to the measure of the full stature of Christ" (Eph. 4:13). God's process is just a lot slower than we'd like, both for ourselves and for the world.

I once sat listening to one biblical prophecy after another at an Advent Service of Lessons and Carols. As voice after voice proclaimed the good news that nation would someday not lift up sword against nation, that deserts would bloom, that trees of the forest would rejoice in God's justice, all I could think of were the ecological disasters everywhere. Such a lovely dream and such grim facts. As if from a deep moan somewhere in my belly came the thought, *We need saving! Some force or power must help turn us from this destruction.* So secular and serious was my reflection that it took a minute or two to realize where I was and what I was listening to. "Savior" was the theme of Advent. But could God really save the world? Not just in theory, doctrine, and ritual but so that the trees could "sing for joy before the LORD" when God comes to bring justice to the earth (see Ps. 96:12-13, RSV)? I had been brought up to believe God could save souls—but a whole planet?

On the way home from church that day, I popped Paul Winter's jazz mass *Missa Gaia* into the tape deck and played the "Agnus Dei," which opens with the sound of whales singing in the deep. I wept as I drove along, humming with the human voices that echoed the whale song. I prayed aloud, "Strong Lamb of God, take away the sin of the world! Help this beautiful, difficult planet. Turn us away from our destructive ways. Please!" In my heart, it was as if I heard a quiet voice respond: "How much do you want this salvation?" My journal's entry for that night records it:

> How much do you want this salvation?
> Enough to love life so much you really don't want
>   to see it harmed?

> Enough to enter
>   still more deeply into the agony of this time in history?
> Enough to tap root yourself deeply
> into the sufficiency of My own active goodness?
> Enough to trust it, love it, cultivate it with all your heart,
>   all your soul, all your might?
> Enough to let it grow you strong enough
>   to join Me in the struggle?

"Death and resurrection aren't a matter of jolly daffodils pushing up in the spring," said the seriously intellectual preacher on the subsequent Good Friday. On the way to the service, I'd just noticed the incredibly strong, sharp blade of the daffodil in my front lawn, dirty from its push through hard soil. I wondered how the highly urban preacher knew so much about what it feels like to be a daffodil. Slicing through the hard soil in an early thaw, risking a sudden freeze, slightly cut by a sharp rock, the daffodil seemed worthy enough as a companion to the story of resurrection.[8]

Perhaps I resented the preacher's jaunty dismissal of the determination of daffodils because I had learned to feel within myself something of what I saw in the daffodils—a power within, stirring, pushing through, helping me to climb out and stand up after every discouragement or defeat. I was brought up to think of saving power as deliverance from beyond. I now clear realized that the gracious goodness touching me from beyond myself was awakening the mysterious gift of health at the core of my being. Both the outer grace and the awakening inner grace were from the same Source, giving me courage to face the path, wherever it might lead:

> Like plants' tendrils crawling out
> from under winter's darkening leaf cover,
> cracking open the hard soil of frozen days,
> thirsting for the light, we seek for You
> not realizing you are the power

which raises us to the search itself.
All along You are there:
already, always and everywhere,
resurrection and life.

Jolly daffodils? Hardly. The green blade of the daffodil that pushes out toward the sun does so only by the power of last year's sunlight patiently savored and stored, day by day, in its very heart.

For a meditation to use in times of depression, see Exercises 2 and 5 in the appendix.

CHAPTER 10

Holy and Glorious Flesh

The Challenge of Sexual Enticement

The Way of Christ invites us to offer our "bodies as a living sacrifice" (Rom. 12:1). The very phrase may make the body shudder. Living sacrifice? Ideas that fly in the face of all reasonable modern notions about healthy emotional life may rise in our minds: flesh-hatred, the repression of desire, and the separation of body and spirit. In a culture where people increasingly regard the body as a pleasure machine, this ancient call to sacrifice sounds alien, off-putting, and even foreboding.

But the "living sacrifice" is not about getting to God by avoiding the body. Rather, it is about communing with the Spirit's discernible presence in our own body, the bodies of others, and the body of the world. Sacrifice does not necessarily mean denial but "making holy," the active consecration of our fleshly bodies to spiritual purposes.[1] We are invited to dedicate every part of our bodily urges, yearnings, and capacities to the practice of spiritual aliveness, following the Christ who opened a way to God "through his flesh" (see Heb. 10:20). The result is the gradual transfiguration of the body, not its crucifixion. As we learn how to "glorify God" in our body (1 Cor. 6:20), we can see how our physical desires are not just needs to be met but opportunities to encounter God's goodness, serving God's love here and now. We may even begin to experience moments of the single-minded immersion in the Spirit's presence that makes our very bodies "full of light" (Luke 11:34-36).

THE WAY THROUGH THE FLESH

We can find fullness of life by sanctifying the body because the body is never purely physical. In every moment its muscles, membranes, and nerves ripple in tangible expression of heart and mind. From angry grimace to beaming smile, from cold shoulder to supportive touch, the flesh is a medium of the soul's utterance.

Soul speaks to soul through the body. The body is our "tent of meeting" with others and the world, lending a deep intimacy to every encounter as we commune and communicate with others. Primal feelings voice themselves through the set of the body, the play of fine muscles in the face, the spray of our body odor, and the subtle but tangible physical energy of our presence. We may know the experience of picking up another's anger first in the pit of our stomach before our eyes find it in the face or our ears hear it from the voice. We may know the joy of sensing that a loved one has come to stand behind us—our body, like radar, picking up the affectionate presence.

Popular modern culture, until recently, has operated on a rather hydraulic image of the body as a set of pressures that need relieving and urges that need expressing; without such release, the body won't work in a healthy manner. Scripture describes the body as something much more. The body is the doorway to a complex mystery of interwoven flesh, soul, and spirit; God works the highest spiritual purposes through the vessel of the flesh.

Hebrew and Greek Scriptures, as well as other ancient traditions, regard the flesh as the "dwelling place" of thoughts, feelings, and spiritual energies that express themselves specially through various areas of the body.[2] Like a great pipe organ with many ranks of pipes, the body utters the music of soul and spirit in different tones and timbres.

- The heart region is experienced as the place where both thoughts and feelings occur: "Mary . . . pondered them in her heart" (Luke 2:19).

- The solar plexus or kidney region ("the reins" in Elizabethan English) is identified with will, intention, and dedication: "Examine me, . . . try my reins and my heart" (Ps. 26:2, KJV).

- The bowels are known as the seat of compassion: "his bowels did yearn upon his brother" (Gen. 43:30, KJV); "I long after you all in the bowels of Jesus" (Phil. 1:8, KJV). The region is also identified with a womblike capacity for mercy in God, women, and men, which nurtures and loves us into fullness of life.[3]

- The loins, legs, and feet form a complex in which vigorous strength—physical and sexual—is experienced: "Gird up now thy loins" (Job 38:3, KJV); "Kings shall come out of thy loins" (Gen. 35:11, KJV); "By my God I can leap over a wall" (Ps. 18:29); "He made my feet like the feet of a deer, and set me secure on the heights" (Ps. 18:33).

- The head is where these energies find vocal and facial expression, the mouth giving voice to the soul: "I will speak in the anguish of my spirit" (Job 7:11) and the face making the inner state visible: Jonathan put honey in his mouth, "and his eyes brightened" (1 Sam. 14:27). Sometimes the crown of glory with which God blesses humans (Ps. 8:5) becomes visible, as when "the skin of [Moses'] face was shining" after his encounter with God (Exod. 34:30) and Christ's face shone "like the sun" (Matt. 17:2).

Each of these body areas manifests the human spirit, and each can be the portal through which the Holy Spirit's energies touch the physical dimension. The love of God can be "poured into our hearts through the Holy Spirit" (Rom. 5:5), the effects rippling through flesh, reaching out to touch lives through very human hands.

Only a generation ago most educated Western people considered the belief that emotion and spirit manifest themselves in different places in the body to be an exotic, primitive, and even superstitious notion. Today the steady march of mind-body medical research indicates that the ancients were perhaps more observant of what was going on in their own flesh than we have been of late. It has now been discovered that the chemicals of emotion operate not only in the brain but throughout the body, clustering especially at the heart, solar plexus, bowels, and, of course, the head, affecting both muscles and mind. Some researchers feel the importance of these body centers qualifies them as secondary brains where reactions are processed unconsciously. The human spirit (and God's Spirit at work through it) has chemical and muscular footprints![4]

GLORIFYING GOD IN THE BODY

Because the physical body is first and foremost a spiritual mystery, it can be a "tent of meeting" with God. On the simplest level, we begin by accepting our bodies as naturally good and wholesome in God's sight, giving thanks for being a physical self. Jewish morning prayers dating from early Christian times begin with thanksgiving for the gift of breath, body, and the capacity to go to the bathroom![5] "Bless to me each thing mine eye sees," prayed the Celtic soul, "each odour . . . each taste"[6] God can use any physical, emotional, or spiritual goodness to invite our pleasure to become praise.

As we learn to link simple pleasure in goodness with a sense of God's goodness, we can tackle the more turbulent tides of the body's life: anger, needy desire, erotic arousal, and other urges that need skillful handling. "Sanctifying" means linking something to God's Spirit. The arousal of any energy, psychological or physical, is meant to be directed by spiritual intention. As the English mystic and poet Charles Williams writes, "Any human energy . . . is capable of being assumed into sacramental and transcendental heights—such is the teaching of the Incarnation."[7]

Does needy desire or erotic arousal stir in my heart and belly? Either of these can drive me impulsively; the energy can turn in on itself, tightening into a knot of aching need and a grinding compulsion to act, do, possess: gotta-have-it, gotta-do-it, gotta-get-it, gotta-gotta-now-gotta![8] Or I can take those "ten deep breaths" of traditional emotional self-control and refrain from acting out a compulsion. I can allow the impulse into awareness, savor and feel it through, and let it speak itself fully, not hiding it from myself or from God. Then I can ask for wisdom on how to direct the impulse to some appropriate purpose and expression that furthers the Good. In so doing, I can link the fire of my body's life with God's presence and purposes. Everything in me moves—in fits and starts—toward serving the divine agape, God's wholehearted and compassionate love for every creature. Each moment of arousal becomes more likely to change into a meeting with God.

A spiritual directee I'll call Stephen recently shared a journal entry about one such occasion. He wrote the following:

> I am standing at the entrance to the Metropolitan
> Museum of Art surveying the crowd surging along Fifth
> Avenue when suddenly someone catches the corner of
> my eye and turns me around. She is still five hundred feet
> away, just one among hundreds, but her saunter, like a
> sleek cat, radiates out from her and touches me like an
> invisible light. My whole body suddenly keen with
> anticipation, eyes unable to turn away from the way her
> black curls cascade as she lopes along, her beauty opens
> my heart. As I retreat before her advance into the
> Museum, I find myself, shy and spellbound, half behind a
> pillar, my body alert as an animal sniffing the air, my soul
> naked and vulnerable in the grip of the fascination, my
> heart aching with longing for closer approach to this

Beauty. It is sheer grace to be closer to the curve of her
neck and the strong line of her jaw. I am transfigured,
not with lust but adoration: *O my God! How beautiful.* I do
not need to "have" her in any way; beholding is enough,
and indeed, all that is possible, granted the circumstances
and my own committed relationship. Finally, a bit afraid
to be thought staring, I tear my eyes away from her,
walking away, carrying the flame of her image inside—
a flame which warms me with love for life every time I
remember it.

Being stunned by beauty or lured by bodies we pass on the
street is not all that unusual for many of us, though we may not
readily admit to it or may pass off such moments as mere animal lust. Such moments of psychophysical arousal, erotic or otherwise, are the target of the call to offer the body and all its
energies in living consecration to the Lord of life: "Bless to me
. . . each lure that tempts my will," as the Celtic prayer puts it.[9]
Well aware of the erotic roots of his experience, Stephen has
chosen to learn how to let eros—our capacity to be aroused by
and connected with the world around us—expand into delight
and appreciation rather than constrict into mere sexual craving.
Nor is this simply a matter of reaction to great beauty. The eros
that connects us to any beloved person, place, or thing—whether
it be a child, a friend, a house, or a job—can become posses-
sively binding or open up into an act of agape.

If few erotic moments are full of such exalted sentiment, it may
be because this way through the flesh has been so little urged
upon us. Stephen's response results from many years of practicing appreciation rather than cultivating lust. As such, it is profoundly obedient to Jesus' call away from craven lusting in your
heart (see Matt. 5:28). Arousal becomes delight in the other and
praise to the Giver of Beauty rather than fantasies of possession.

There is a safer way, of course; it is the one ordinarily followed
in conventional religion: When tempted by the arousal of desire,

keep your head down, your eyes to yourself, and banish every hint of desire from the mind. While this approach safeguards the truth that those on the Way are not free to "act out" their impulses and whims all over the landscape, it threatens whole sections of the self with exclusion from the process of sanctification. A strong commitment to responsible restraints in outer behavior can be combined with a patient, compassionate awareness of the inner cauldron of the body's heart and mind. Through that dual action, every aspect of the soul and body becomes available to God, every small energy seeks its link to the great, loving energy of God.

At its heart, redemption, not suppression, is the Christian way: "Whatever is not embraced cannot be redeemed."[10] Everything in us mysteriously "rises to the in-Godding,"[11] united with the "in-Godded" Humanity of Christ. All our desires and energies, even lust, will in the end break out of their current unripe and problematic state of development and become mature aspects of our nature. As we saw in chapter 8, anger will become the holy wrath that protects all that is precious and good; envy will become admiration and worship; lust will break the bonds of its tight, self-centered coil and become fully related eros—adoring connection with the glory pervading all creation.

THE TRANSFIGURATION OF THE BODY

It may now be clearer why Scripture asserts that "the body is meant . . . for the Lord, and the Lord for the body" (1 Cor. 6:13). Every bodily energy exists to lead us into contact with God in every earthly thing and to love every earthly thing in God. Our very flesh slowly regains its "unbroken character" of flesh-soul-Spirit unity and becomes "God-receiving."[12] Through the sanctification of our erotic capacity to behold, delight, and connect, we discover relations between ourselves and the world "permeated with the spirit of love; . . . in love with everything, with a love . . . present as a pervasive atmosphere . . . an unconscious background to every relation in life, even the holiest."[13] When such love pervades a life, the effects are often physically tangible, making one a more gracious presence for others.

"I don't quite know what's happening," said a woman who practices this Way. "Utter strangers smile at me on the street and say 'hello' as if they knew me." I understood part of the mystery. Her deep and interested love for life makes her—body and soul—alive to life's simple beauties and deep frustrations. Her face often radiates with a benign smile—not fixed like the ruthlessly cheerful person but soft, pliant, unaffected. Her eyes, in this state, are not worried or preoccupied but sparkling with a contemplative, noninvasive interest. People simply find themselves drawn to this physical-spiritual presence.

Many stories throughout Christian history relate how far such a transformation of the body may go. Eyewitnesses observed Francis of Assisi, Ignatius of Loyola, Francis de Sales, and Seraphim of Moscow all surrounded by brilliant light while preaching or engaged in worship. The light that shone around Giles of Assisi was so great that it obscured the moonlight, according to the witnesses.[14] Such stories exist not only about medieval marvels. I knew a priest who once went on retreat with friends at a Trappist monastery. Getting lost on the large property, they called to a workman in the field for directions. "As the young man turned and began to walk toward us," Father Austin said, "we all fell silent, awestruck, because he was radiating a barely perceptible but very tangible light. He gave directions like any ordinary person, then turned back to his task, still shining. When we came to the Mother House, we stammered out our astonishment to the guest master, who just laughed and said, 'O yes, that would be Brother G.'"[15]

The goal of a spiritual life is not dramatic physical manifestations as such but rather the state of soul and body out of which they come. Such manifestations signal something available to everyone—God's own smile illuminating heart, mind, and flesh. My smiling friend concludes her puzzled musing about the effect of her presence in the world: "And I seem destined to be the one that short, elderly ladies in the supermarket seek out in a crowd to get something beyond their reach."

Small matters. Merely the body of ordinary life, tangibly transfigured.

CHAPTER 11

Busyness and Sabbath Time

I'm so busy now with work that simply has to be done," said the businesswoman in our spiritual sharing group, "that I can't really grow spiritually." Everyone nodded. "It's not that I don't have a spiritual life; it's just in maintenance mode, marking time till I can stop just coping. I need a break—just as soon as this next thing is finished."

What so possesses us that we can't stop until "this next thing is finished"? Many inward factors affect us, but one overwhelming outer factor grips our inward parts: the drumbeat of the marketplace relentlessly pervades areas of life once hallowed by a break from the everyday. The weekend gives way, in a flextime world, to business seven days a week. The string of three-day federal holidays quickly fills with business as usual, hyped by "sale" signs, dragooning millions of consumers—and employees—into work, thus abandoning even former Sabbath breaks of weekend and holiday. "Time off" from this task-oriented world exists increasingly as an individualized rather than a communal experience; and that time off may be punctuated by work carted about on laptop computers and beeping its way through cell phones into leisure time. Only "The Holidays" between Thanksgiving and New Year's still have the power to make ordinary time stop, inviting a different spirit; yet even that period easily becomes overstuffed and busy.

There's nothing wrong with what the Book of Common Prayer calls "honorable industry."[1] Our harried administrator confesses that she enjoys her work, which helps accomplish worthy goals in the community. It's just that having "the next thing" always breathing down our necks eventually poisons both body and soul.

"Take a break," God says to ancient Israel: a real break, an absolute break from the workaday world, not just for your sake but for the whole family and tribe—wife, servants, children, and animals as well. "Six days shall work be done, but on the seventh day you shall have a holy sabbath of solemn rest to the LORD" (Exod. 35:2). Why? "Even I took a break when I'd worked six days," says God. "If I need a break, you think you don't?"[2]

The importance of such Sabbath time came home to me with real force recently. One Monday morning, on my "day off," it became crystal clear during meditation that "Remember the Sabbath day, and keep it holy"—that is, one day in seven free from work—was actually a commandment.[3] It was an order, directed point-blank at me, for my soul's health: Thou shalt take a break. So I did, for the most part, for a while. I consecrated Sunday evenings and Mondays as Sabbath time, not just from work but for my soul to have rest and renewal in a good book, more time for meditation and prayer, a leisurely lunch with my wife, a long walk, perhaps some time with a friend, maybe an evening of music and conversation.

That routine lasted until the next fall when I was invited to do a series of eight Monday-morning lectures on Scripture to 250 leisure learners in a distant suburb. Since I couldn't turn down such a gratifying opportunity, there went Monday mornings. I assured myself that I'd take the rest of the day off, of course. But as I was already busy on Mondays, the many "next things to do" somehow managed to squeeze in a visit on Monday afternoons. My mistake (or shall I call it disobedience?) was not that I let Mondays go but that I did not claim another day for the Sabbath the Lord had commanded.

And I paid for my mistake. By early November I was feeling burdened. By Thanksgiving I felt so overburdened that the thought of putting up the Christmas tree—usually a special occasion—held no allure. But I was still "fast bound in schedule" (or was it sin?) and could not "set myself free," as a traditional Lutheran confession puts it. Only the death of my father, the straw that broke the camel's back, finally made ordinary time stop. My usual leisurely post-Christmas vacation became an enforced Sabbath of mourning and sickness, as weary body and soul forcibly made a separation between the workaday world and the realm of sacred restoration.

THE SHAPE OF SABBATH: SOUL TIME FOR RELATIONSHIPS

As both the rabbinical tradition and Jesus knew, "the sabbath was made for humankind," for our health and well-being (Mark 2:27).[4] The Sabbath is to be holy in the sense of separated— a time intentionally set apart from the ordinary push-pull of work and family tasks. The sole purpose of the separation is to consecrate that time for maintenance, renewal, and the soul's progress.

That the Sabbath was "made for us" is manifest in the care taken by traditional Jews to create on this day a sheltered space for cultivating relationship with family and friends, with the ancestral wisdom, and with God. Far from an austere day defined by forbidden activities,the Sabbath is a leisurely, festive time of food, song, conversation, study, and enjoyment. Sabbath invites soul and body to bask in the goodness of life with God—beginning with a bath! "I couldn't imagine greeting the Sabbath without a bath and fresh, clean clothes," confesses a rabbi friend of mine.[5] In traditional communities, people leave work early to wash and dress themselves for the arrival of what they see as a welcoming of a holy, intimate presence into the human circle. During the late-afternoon prayers at synagogue, they sing a special hymn hailing the Sabbath as a Queen, the manifestation of God's nearer presence among us.[6]

Before sundown the home has been decked out for a special dinner. The dining room has become a holy place, a temple ready for the indwelling of God's presence in the community. After sundown, candles are lit to signal crossing a definite, sacred line into the shelter of Sabbath time. From this moment on, no work is allowed—even unfinished tasks! Food for the evening and next day is already prepared, soiled dishes can be stacked to await the end of the Sabbath, and every aspect of domestic labor except the literal serving of food and resetting of the table can be avoided. Why? Out of some legalistic superstition that "work" will incur divine displeasure? Not at all. These arrangements allow one the freedom for much fuller attention to the pleasures of the time together.

The family gathers to celebrate in song, gesture, and prayer all the vital fabric of community that makes and keeps life human. Family members bless God for creating the world and calling Israel; the husband blesses the wife for her sacred ministry of nurture and industry; the parents bless the children in order that they grow wise and strong; everyone invites the angels to "come and dwell among us"; and each person greets the others with the blessing *Shabbat shalom*—"Sabbath peace." Dinner proceeds with conversation and singing long after the food is finished. All task-oriented conversation is banned, so that everyone can dedicate the time to talking about God, wisdom in living, and people's lives.

Saturday morning traditionally brings the major liturgical service at the synagogue. Like most worship until the modern era, the service lasts two to three hours, a leisurely basking in familiar and beloved worship forms that is now a lost cultural art. People meander with God, the mind at play in the fields of psalm and song, ancient prayers interspersed with the soaring, soul-piercing melodies of the cantor. These lengthy ritual actions create the time necessary for the letting go that must precede the letting in of holy words and the letting be of God's presence.

The Sabbath midday meal is, again, a leisurely affair with conversation (like the old-fashioned Christian Sunday dinner). Afternoon prayers and a nap follow. Then comes relaxed family time—a stroll, time with the children, conversation with family or friends. One sees in any predominantly Jewish neighborhood whole families out together for a Sabbath walk, sauntering slowly along in laughter and conversation, going no place in a hurry.

In the later afternoon the family engages in study time, reading and discussing Torah wisdom, and then come evening prayers. At sundown, the simple, solemn, decisive ritual of Havdalah—"separation"—is celebrated, often with a larger group of visiting family or friends. A braided candle flares like a small torch; a brief chant thanks God for all the "separations" or "borders" that keep life whole and healthy: between light and darkness, festival and workday, the Sabbath and ordinary time. A plaintive traditional hymn addressed to Elijah yearns for the coming of Messiah—for the day when God's desires will be honored fully by humankind, and life itself will bask in the fuller presence of God. Then the flame is dramatically doused in wine, and the Sabbath is over! We have crossed a sacred line back into ordinary time, where ordinary occupations may be resumed as a way of serving God in the world. Even then, people may linger, seeking to "carry the fragrance" of the Sabbath into the week.

The New Testament says we are not meant to be "weary in well doing" (2 Thess. 3:13, KJV). Judaism still remembers how to prevent this weariness. The Sabbath, fully observed, is said to give a person a "second soul," that is, to make us twice as rich, deep, and large as we were at the end of the workweek.

APPLICATIONS OF SABBATH WISDOM

What wisdom might modern spiritual pilgrims, especially Christians—who have no obligation to keep Israel's ritual laws—learn from these rich traditions about keeping Sabbath time in our lives?

1. *A weekly day of separation from tasks.* The most straightforward obedience to the wisdom of Sabbath would be to reclaim the Christian celebration of Sunday as "the Lord's Day" and to focus it, as do the Jews, on an ordered time for taking care of our relationship to self, family, friends, and God. (Seventh-Day Adventists and a few other Christian groups have moved their holy day to Saturday in order to reclaim the ancient Sabbath time.)

Tilden Edwards's *Sabbath Time* contains suggestions for a Christian Lord's Day celebration that begins with Saturday evening supper and goes through early Sunday evening, with worship in the morning, a midday meal, and a Sabbathlike afternoon of family and friends. Family games, an excursion to the country, reading books aloud together, singing, and even dancing—all these make for some real, quality soul time. The day might end with a family prayer service, either from a set liturgy or devised by the family.[7]

In our marketplace world, however, such a full-day Sabbath observance is not always feasible. I hear more and more stories about people in the lower or lower-middle income brackets who receive an ultimatum: work on Sunday or lose your job. (Jews, of course, have always faced this dilemma about Saturdays in a predominantly Christian culture.) Ministers and church professionals too may not find Sunday to be their greatest day of rest. All the more reason, therefore, to carve out another day. My wife and I have had some success with our consecrated Sunday evening through Monday night Sabbaths, with time apart and together. Without this time, we end up losing track of each other, our souls, and our capacity to "taste and see" that both life and God are, in fact, very good (see Ps. 34:8).

2. *Leisurely worship.* Sabbath time gives space for unhurried prayer, privately or with others. One of my deepest experiences of corporate worship came during a Sabbath conference led by my friend Rabbi Shefa Gold, who sees in the traditionally

leisurely Sabbath worship Judaism's form of contemplative prayer. She said, "The whole service is a preparation to be able to say the Shema, 'Hear, O Israel, the LORD our God, the LORD is one" (Deut. 6:4, NIV) with our whole heart, mind, and strength. That's why we need a long time to prepare: time to cultivate the heart space to focus deeply on the reality of God's Oneness that unites all things in the cosmos."[8] And so we did, spending two hours in chant and discussion and meditative prayer. After the high point of the Shema, we read the Torah-portion for the day. Never before had I heard the words of Scripture sound so alive! Just hearing them felt like food to the soul. Why? Because the ears of our hearts were opened by leisurely worship. The memory of that experience makes me yearn for public worship services less rushed, more full of song and prayer.

3. *Vacation, retreat, and holiday.* Ancient peoples, including Israel, didn't take vacations; they celebrated holy days and festival seasons. Soul time needs to be celebrated throughout the year, not just lumped into "The Holidays." Claiming some special days through the year as Sabbath time for self or family gives everyone something to look forward to. My wife and I have created our own calendar related to both church and secular year: Advent candles and calendar before Christmas; early spring flowers for Candlemas on February 2 to break the winter gloom; a special afternoon and evening around Valentine's Day; small gatherings on secular holidays like Memorial Day and Labor Day, with some mealtime prayers related to the spiritual dimension of the occasion; and an annual costume party held variously on Twelfth Night to end Christmastide, Mardi Gras, April Fools' Day, Midsummer Eve, Hallowe'en. Entertaining linked with a sacred theme gives an added flavor to the day, influences conversation, and helps create ritual without turning the day oppressively pious. Such occasions would also be good opportunities to teach younger children the values of one's civilization and take an added day of Sabbath rest together. For years, my wife's

family—descended from French Huguenot stock—celebrated a lighthearted and festive family day on August 24, Saint Bartholomew's Day, the anniversary of the infamous massacre when so many French Protestants were martyred by the Catholic monarchy. In our celebration (inspired by the festive Jewish partying at Purim, the festival of deliverance) we sang a French hymn, told a simple version of the tale, with hisses for the wicked French queen and hurrahs for the ancestors who were delivered, and a genuine prayer of thanks for the family's life. (One Roman Catholic nun we knew begged for an invitation so she could hiss the wicked queen too!)

We've even, on occasion, consecrated a day or two of our vacation as retreat time, going into silence for meandering prayer, reading, meditation, and simple worship together. I myself have come to see our extended family vacations as chances to do my own personal spiritual practice in community. Free from the push and pull of phone calls, deadlines to meet, and clients who demand my attention, I am free to practice "being here now," as fully present to each activity and each person as I can be. Sabbath leisure for Centering Prayer on the beach blends beautifully with being able to throw myself fully into sand-castle making, card playing, fish grilling, or in-law listening, as occasion demands. A week or more of Sabbath time brings sheer pleasure, when the time "vacated" from work is intentionally, inwardly consecrated to savoring the quality and presence of human soul and Holy Spirit.

The fruit of such observances is nothing less than the "second soul" that tradition promises to Israel on the Sabbath. It's hard to describe the resonance—an inaudible but virtually physical "hum" that begins to emerge in a group that has entered into such separated, protected, sheltered time and space. Perhaps the ageless rhythms of body time simply begin to predominate over the jerky, forced physical reactions of our culture's increasingly pressured work time. Perhaps the deep inner self—the soul—has a chance to breathe, connect, and be in touch, when not measured out by the slots in an appointment book. Or perhaps it is simply true that, given half a chance, some space to dwell among us, and an actual invitation, God's nearer presence settles in for a visit.

CHAPTER 12

The Dangers of Affluence

Craving in a Consumerist Culture

My godson's second birthday party was a typically festive suburban event: adoring relatives, well-wishing friends, a bevy of boisterous toddlers, and an avalanche of gifts. At first glance, Ian seemed overjoyed at the twenty or more brightly wrapped packages, tearing into them with lusty abandon. But as the ritual of abundance went on, he became increasingly ill at ease. No sooner had one gift been unwrapped than another was being shoved in his face. A crisis began to brew when he opened a set of plastic Winnie-the-Pooh figures that clearly captured his heart. He wanted to stop, take these figures, and play with them. But ritual is ritual, and the gift unwrapping went on. Ian became increasingly unhappy and spaced-out, overwhelmed by the sheer volume of color, sound, stimulation, and items to be interested in. He got cranky, almost on the verge of tears. "He's just tired," opined the happy adults around him as the ritual ended.

I felt otherwise. I had seen the moment when Ian wanted to stop and explore the sheer delight of Winnie-the-Pooh. So I sidled up to the child, who was drunk with too-muchness, and presented the Pooh figures to him again. Did he want to play with Pooh? Did he ever! While the party swirled around us, we sat quietly at the living room coffee table arranging figures as he slowly calmed down and became focused and happy again, connected with a toy that had called out to him for exploration and enjoyment.

As I saw it, Ian had just been baptized into the perils of affluence. It was an experience he, as a suburban American kid from a family with a decent income, would have again and again: being so overwhelmed with "stuff" that it snuffs out the capacity to explore and enjoy the simple goodness of creation.

The whole incident forcefully reminded me of a chilling sequence about chimpanzee greed I had seen on a TV documentary about the work of Jane Goodall. Ordinarily chimps are fairly laid back about their food gathering and eating as well as reasonably cooperative with one another. On the rare occasions when they hunt animals, they engage in a ritual of sharing the kill. On the occasion recorded in the documentary, Goodall's assistants had secured a shipment of bananas for the wild chimps to facilitate making observations. The chimps, however, caught sight of this unprecedented abundance and broke into the camp to take advantage of it. A mountain of bananas! Who in Chimpdom had ever seen such a wonder? This affluence propelled the chimps on an uncharacteristic rampage of frenzied desire, interpersonal conflict, and aggressive possessiveness. Forget the little daily moments of shared nuts and termites. Forget the ritual of sharing the kill. It was every chimp for himself or herself. It was the first time in their chimpanzee lives that they had ever encountered Mammon. An alpha male quickly took possession of the miraculous pile of bananas and fended off all the others, screeching at the top of his lungs, gobbling one banana after another, barely noticing what he was doing. In traditional Christian terms, he had been overcome by concupiscence—unbridled, untamed, unredeemed desire.

The chimp wasn't happy. All through the terrible screeching, some other part of his chimp soul kept reaching out with his arm and index finger to touch the finger of the closest screeching chimp, as if that touch might restore him and the other to the social and spiritual sanity they had temporarily lost.

Our cultural worship of what the poet e.e. cummings called "much and quick" (in his poem "jehovah buried, satan dead") prevents us from finding the soul satisfaction our bodies and brains are designed to find in being with the objects, creatures, and adventures available in the world around us. Typically we attribute this dilemma to our being "too materialistic," but the truth is that our consumer-driven culture doesn't appreciate matter very much at all. "Much and quick" are ways we use matter— extravagantly, wastefully, and destructively. No society that genuinely loved matter would treat it as disrespectfully as we do.

God, according to the story the Bible tells, likes matter a lot. God births a world teeming with abundance and beauty, redolent with shape and form and finds it *tov*—not just "good," as most translations have it, but "delectable, delightful, desirable" (see Gen. 1:10, 12, 18, 21, 25, 31). Just as the great fireball of energy that erupted from the big bang seems to have naturally granulated into matter, so the Divine seems naturally bent on materializing its hopes and dreams. And far from being told to shun the sinuous beauty of earth, humans are called to share God's delight, joining the song of all creation:

> Glorify the Lord, O chill and cold,
>
> . . . .
>
> Drops of dew and flakes of snow,
>
> . . . .
>
> O shining light and enfolding dark.
> . . . O springs of water, seas, and streams.
> —"A Song of Creation," 1979 BCP, 88

Not only does God like matter, but God seems exuberant about abundance. The Genesis story dwells lovingly on how the waters bring forth "swarms of living creatures" and "every living creature . . . of every kind" (Gen. 1:20-21). I think of this passage every spring as the silver maple in front of my house showers us with twirling thousands of seedpods. Such extravagance! Such diverse usefulness: as new maple seedlings, as food for animals, as compost for the soil. An ancient Hebrew blessing expresses this robust sense of the goodness of fruitful abundance:

> Blessed shall be the fruit of your womb, the fruit of your ground, and the fruit of your livestock, . . . the increase of your cattle. . . .
> Blessed shall be your basket and your kneading bowl. . . .
> The LORD will command the blessing upon you in your barns, and in all that you undertake; he will bless you in the land that the LORD your God is giving you.
> —Deuteronomy 28:4-5, 8

Yes, Scripture also pictures the Divine as implacably opposed to unjust gain (Ezek. 22:13), hoarding (Luke 12:15-21), or letting the craving for possession rule one's life (Matt. 6:24). But these problems do not arise from the stuff of the world itself; they arise from the human psyche driven mad by seeing a pile of bananas. It cannot be stressed too strongly that abundance itself comes from God, who "gives . . . power to get wealth" (Deut. 8:18).

What's wrong with our modern glut of consumer goods is that it bars the way to the true use and enjoyment of the fruitful abundance celebrated in Scripture. Little Ian's unhappy, overstimulated face demonstrated the proof of this wisdom. A soul-constricting *spirituality* drives our consumerist rituals, a spirituality that panders shamelessly to the desire for continually increasing possession, the fantasy of limitless pleasure, and the need for status. It was this spirituality that all of us adults were, albeit unconsciously, foisting upon Ian in a ritual designed as much to train him how to be a good consumer as to express our love for him. We didn't mean it that way. But our sensibilities have been forcefully shaped by nonstop magazine and TV commercials proclaiming the good news that we can find satisfaction in possession, accumulation, and consumption rather than in learning how to relate to matter with respect, savoring it with pleasure. As the ancient wisdom in Scripture long since observed: "The lover of money will not be satisfied with money; nor the lover of wealth, with gain" (Eccles. 5:10).

Affluence as we currently practice it doesn't use abundance well, either wisely for ourselves or justly in relation to other people. The glut of affluence flows through the lives of the privileged accompanied by a siren call to unbridled, unceasing craving that constantly threatens the blessing inherent in good things. This glut also shapes the desires of many less privileged, who are bidden by this false gospel to want nothing more than their share of this overstuffed pie.

How can those of us who bask in affluence liberate our God-given capacities to delight in the goodness of the world from the seductive corruption of our affluence? And, just as crucially, how can that enjoyment become a springboard to a more generous and just sharing of the earth's goods with others?

APPRECIATIVE ENJOYMENT

We need to tackle the misuse of abundance at its source: craving. Craving differs from simple need or desire. Craving is that cramped, sometimes hurting feeling of "gotta have, gotta have." It is a hand reaching out, tense and aggressive, to grab rather than open to receive.

Many "spiritual" circles lump together craving and simple desire and define the cure as the denial of desire. Much Christian spirituality through the ages has vehemently opposed what Freud called the "pleasure principle." That stance has been based on suspicions of the senses' lure and discomfort with the body's exquisite capacities for pleasure. Hair shirts, mixing ashes in one's food to take away any good taste, self-flagellation, and prudish self-restraint in simple pleasures—extreme but widespread practices through the ages—seem odd ways to follow a Master whose delight in dinner parties caused his soured critics to slander him as a "glutton and a drunkard" (Matt. 11:19).

The cure for craving—appreciative enjoyment—involves embracing our senses rather than shunning them. "Sustain me with raisins, refresh me with apples," says the Song of Solomon (2:5), the Bible's great feast of delight in the pleasure of the senses. If we stay in touch with the body itself, its sensations and reactions as we eat, for example, we will enjoy each bite of food more and will be less likely to overeat. We disarm craving by wisely fulfilling desire.

Fighting the flesh-denying tendency that eventually took such strong hold in Christian circles, the New Testament says, "For everything created by God is good, and nothing is to be rejected, provided it is received with thanksgiving" (1 Tim. 4:4).

A friend once reported that while on retreat at a monastery, he had been fascinated by one monk who always ate with chopsticks. At the end of his retreat, my friend had asked the monk whether this habit indicated interest in things Asian, perhaps connected with study of Asian spirituality. "Not at all," said the monk. "The chopsticks slow me down so I pay attention to my food."

I really love to lead people in an exercise of meditative or "sacred" eating that I learned years ago from a teacher of sensory awareness. Over simple appetizers, we practice being fully present with our senses to each appetizer in turn. We each take a pistachio nut and examine it lovingly, noticing the color and texture of the shell, then slowly cracking it open, putting the nut in our mouth, rolling its salted surface around in our mouth and then slowly, very slowly, beginning to chew it. People are almost always astonished at the burst of nutty flavor produced by this first bite and the reaction from the whole mouth, which rushes to meet the taste with its own sweet moisture. (In fact, people are surprised at how clean and sweet their own saliva is!) Finally they are intrigued by how many different levels of subtly changing flavor the small pistachio nut puts forth as they chew it with full awareness.

We follow the same procedure with other foodstuffs: a bit of parsley or strong greens like arugula for contrast, a strawberry to experience tart and sweet together, and then a fragrant loaf of bread broken and shared to initiate the meal proper. When the main course arrives, people express amazement at how pleasurably *satisfied* they already feel and how spontaneously grateful. As we begin the main course in silence, resuming a more normal pace, people are urged to stay in touch with taste and touch and smell. So often, when we devour something and then think, *It's so good I've just got to have more,* we haven't allowed ourselves to take full pleasure in what we've already eaten.

At the end of one of these meals, one participant sighed, "This has been so enjoyable I hate to think of going back to the real world." Another spoke up immediately, "I think maybe *this* is the real world." Since we so often eat our ideas of food rather than the food itself, an attentive, appreciative exercise such as this brings us "back to our senses," back into the world of God's own making and out of our needy fantasies.

ENJOYING AND LETTING GO

We can apply a similar method of appreciative enjoyment to any object, creature, location, or experience we encounter. I used to dislike window-shopping intensely, thus rejecting an experience I could share with my wife. Meandering about looking at things one wasn't going to buy, and worse yet, seeing items one couldn't afford seemed silly and useless. The meditative eating exercise taught me to approach such artifacts with a different attitude: I could experience pleasure in a beautiful, clever, or well-designed object without having to possess it. Suddenly our occasional forays into window-shopping became occasions of feasting: "Look at this! Isn't that beautiful!" Instead of focusing on emptiness and lack, I focused on the quality of the object itself. I could enjoy it for itself, letting go of the need to own it. It is an act of possessing through experience rather than through owning. I leave with a sense of fullness. Paradoxically I learn how to possess without possessing.

Once we do not have to own something to enjoy it, this art of nonpossessive relating opens up the whole world to us. Is this new relationship part of what Saint Paul means by saying that "all things are [ours]" if we "belong to Christ" (see 1 Cor. 3:21-23)? Everything in creation, natural and artificial, can become a personal gift of the Divine to us and to everyone else on the planet—not because we own them but because we can see and respond to them.

FINDING THE SOUL QUALITY OF THINGS

Our souls can speak to us through things that allure us, drawing us to cherish them. In many ways the glut of consumer goods, which the Industrial Revolution made available to people in the developed world, presents a serious barrier to enjoying the "soul quality" of objects. My friend Diana Beach, a therapist in the Jungian tradition, says ancient peoples felt that places and objects could accumulate a "soul charge"—a power to stir and nourish the soul. This intensity, arising out of response to the very nature of places and objects, helps sustain a sense of life's worthwhileness. The ancient Hebrew proverbialist found deep satisfaction in "things too wonderful" to understand: "the way of an eagle in the air; the way of a serpent upon a rock; the way of a ship in the midst of the sea; and the way of a man with a maid" (Prov. 30:18-19, KJV). The sinuous, curvaceous, rolling, tidal quality of all these creatures awakens the soul to the wonder of existence.

This soul nourishment surrounds us in everyday objects. Diana helps people do a "soul-nourishment scan" of their own lives by identifying three of their favorite items of clothing, pieces of music, treasured objects kept through the years, and books that still haunt them. Often the soul value of the object has little to do with its market price. It has to do with an appreciative connectedness—to that worn denim shirt that carries carefree relaxation in its very fabric, the cracked mug you just can't throw out. The relationship is often nothing less than love.

Sometimes we hear our problem defined thusly: we "love things and use people" when we should "love people and use things." We shall be closer to God's own eye of delighted love for the world if we let ourselves love both people and things in their places and "use" each with respect, consideration, and justice.

GIVING THINGS AWAY

As we grow in the habit of nonpossessive enjoyment and use, we may find our resistance to sharing lessens. We feel less need to hoard for ourselves. Enjoyment can lead to the desire to spread the joy.

I had my first lesson in letting go at college when a friend offered to share his fruit salad with me. Because I'd grown up in a home where one certainly didn't eat off others' plates (and in a church where one had one's Communion out of one's own private cup, thank you!), food sharing of this sort startled me. Steve's manner as he shoved that fruit cup across the table at me with a grin and said, "This is really good; have the rest of it," somehow revealed to me how giving something away comes easily when it is an overflow of joy.

My most life-changing lesson in letting go occurred when I took a 50-percent cut in pay and faced a serious challenge to make ends meet. Suddenly my wife and I, children of post–World War II affluence, realized how valuable each dollar was to us. To make matters worse, my wife's wisdom tooth broke and she needed an expensive dental crown. We literally did not have the money for it and were fortunate to have a dentist who let us pay in installments. Every penny was precious.

One day during that period, as I drove through a poor neighborhood on my way home, I thought, *What about people who can't get their teeth fixed? What do they do?* I became aware as never before how fortunate I was. That night my wife and I decided to begin tithing. We recognized the importance of giving money to help people who had much less than we.

Reportedly, lower-income Christians are more likely to give a greater percentage of their money to charity than upper-income believers. Maybe they have a keener sense of how vulnerable one is without the resources to take care of oneself and one's family.

Romanticizing the poor as happier or more virtuous than the rich would be false, but the reality is that generosity sometimes abounds in circumstances of deprivation. Harsh living conditions bring out either the worst or the best in people.

A church youth group I knew had a life-transforming experience encountering poor people in Haiti a few years ago on their annual work-study program. Hailing from one of the richest suburbs in America, these kids at first were shocked, even repelled, by the grinding poverty of the rural Haitian village where they stayed. That was, however, only the first impression. They were bowled over by the people's generosity with the little they had. The village parishioners gave these rich kids from America a simple feast and commonly greeted them with offers of food and drink. The kids were even more disarmed by the natural *joie de vivre* of the village Christians. They, in fact, had never encountered people as basically joyful as these folk. Of course they had sorrows, angers, and difficulties. But underneath all that flourished a simple, grateful joy in appreciating the bare necessities of life: sunlight, rain, air, water, friendship, food. The American youth had grown up in a much more world-weary, driven, hassled social environment where people were always striving to get more than they already possessed and were very conscious of having less than somebody else. The poor villagers had something that the youth were missing. The young people were so astonished by their observations, they insisted on having a special congregational meeting when they returned home to tell their elders about this remarkable discovery.

Such tales are no excuse for complacency with regard to poverty. Grinding poverty degrades as often as it ennobles, and Scripture directs, "Open your hand to the poor and needy neighbor in your land" (Deut. 15:11). But experiences like that of the church youth can help startle us out of the false assumption that affluence and happiness have much to do with each other or that a craving for more will lead to anything remotely resembling joy. Jesus puts this truth very matter-of-factly: "Take care!

Be on your guard against all kinds of greed; for one's life does not consist in the abundance of possessions" (Luke 12:15).

The Divine envisions bounty for everyone—a vision of a world where all have enough to "sit under their own vines and under their own fig trees" (Mic. 4:4), of abundance shared—the opposite of possessive affluence. And the way to that vision is enjoyment shared: "Freely you have received, freely give" (Matt. 10:8, NIV).

I'm a book hoarder in a big way. My therapist friend Diana says my books have a big "soul charge" for me, and this leads to some kind of semiconscious craving to have them around me always. If not pruned regularly, my library begins to invade the house like the wild kudzu vine of the American South.

I shouldn't have been surprised, then, when the Spirit's prompting came to "give your books away." My first reaction, of course, was visceral panic—a threat to whatever unconscious fantasy I entertain about having all these books as soul companions. But as I pondered, I realized I was being asked to stop blocking the flow of this goodness through the world. Why not pass the goodness on? On my next birthday, I invited some friends to dinner and gave each of them a gift of books I thought they might like—the first step in a new habit. The next step was to see the collection as a library open to others.

Why do gifts in our culture have to be new—brand-spanking, fresh-from-the-factory new? Does the god of affluence give a bigger "soul charge" in our minds to the items that keep the wheels of industry moving? What if we gave each other "cherished" treasures rather than "used" things as gifts?

NONPOSSESSIVENESS AND JUSTICE

Our incredibly affluent cultures in the developed world must soon face the fact that the planet will not long support our high-living consumption of its resources. We in the developed world are envied, and increasingly hated, for feasting while much of the world suffers significant deprivation.

The developing world, however, simply cannot replicate the incredible pile of bananas that characterizes suburban living in Europe and North America, because the resources will not exist—for them or for us. We will either choose or be forced to create a simpler, more environmentally sustainable lifestyle. In so doing, we will have an opportunity to join the rest of the world in creating more realistic expectations for human life on this planet.

Those who, even now, begin practicing nonpossessive use of the good things of the earth, who enjoy and let go, who cherish and pass on what they cherish, may be able to demonstrate how to live that simpler lifestyle with grace, peace, and joy.

CHAPTER 13

Christ and Caesar

Taming the Pecking Order

O n a recent Saturday morning, I was under great pressure to get my educational center ready for a big 10:00 event and also to meet a pre-event class at 8:30. One of the class regulars arrived, asked how I was, and, when I said I felt harassed and burdened, replied jokingly, "You? With all your meditation skills and you don't know how to stay calm under pressure?" I responded with the quip, "If I can't do it, that just shows how hard it is." He shot back, "Actually I was going to offer to teach you how!" We both laughed at our bantering game of one-upmanship, and he helped me finish the setup.

This drive to feel superior—in talent, skill, beauty, something—resides deep in human nature. Like the rigid pecking order of bird societies, in which birds with more status get first dibs on territory and food and get pecked less, human beings persistently jockey for status, position, and power every day. Some people express more exaggerated drive than others, but most of us sense concern for a good place in the pecking order as a recurrent preoccupation, even if only as a quiet murmur at the back of our minds.

This reality is demonstrated by how easily most of us become annoyed if someone tries to push in front of us in a line: "I was here first!" Or bulldozes her way in front of us in merging traffic: "Who does she think she is?" Or fails to thank us properly for a favor: "What I did is being discounted!" It shows up in the "comparative suffering" that can be the ugly fallout of an argument or accident: "You hurt me more than I hurt you!" In each of these instances, someone deeply senses a violation of the balance of power.

The pervasive power of the pecking order of status, position, and power reveals itself in our feelings when we see an important politician, movie or TV star in the flesh and especially if we gain access to an "important" person's presence. My friend Mark still remembers vividly the time he entered a restaurant on the sophisticated Upper West Side of Manhattan where a currently hot male movie star was enjoying supper with some friends. "His presence pervaded the whole room. It felt like everyone knew he was there but had to prove their urbanity by ignoring him."

Humans recurrently organize societies on the basis of status, power, and privilege. There's no way around it: Some people possess more power and influence within their social structures than others; they are better connected and can make things happen more easily. But the reality of status faces us all, however high or low our position in the family, at work, in our social circle, or in society. Virtually no one is so low on the pecking order that someone lower cannot be found or at least imagined. Not uncommonly, people who feel "low down" take out their frustrations on people still lower in status. Thus the most ominous expression of the pecking order's spell manifests itself when human beings mistreat those without the status or power to fight back effectively.

One day when Jesus finds his disciples bickering about their relative places in the pecking order—"Which of us is to be regarded as greatest?"—he challenges them to organize the world and their lives in a different way: "The greatest among you must become . . . like one who serves," just as he comes among them as "one who serves" (see Luke 22:24-27). Jesus' way literally turns the pecking order around.

In the ancient pagan world, the "rulers" and "benefactors" hold sway, compelling others to serve their interests. This organization of life around the pecking order is the "mind of Caesar" in whatever society or life it may occur. In contrast, the "mind of Christ" calls us to yield our pecking-order impulse to the service of the reign of God. Jesus doesn't destroy the impulse but calls it to a process of conversion. Acknowledging the fact that "great ones" exist, he calls them to use their power in service to God's purposes in the world.

In other words, Jesus says if we've got power, use it rather than flaunt it. First, we are to dethrone the pecking order in our lives: "Seek first God's reign and righteousness" (Matt. 6:33, RCM). Whoever we are, we are to use our powers, privileges, and abilities—small or great—in cooperation with God's loving purposes for the world: "Let the greatest among you become . . . as the one who serves" (Luke 22:26, RSV). Secondly, Jesus invites us to discover that what needs to be done in the world takes priority over who gets credit for doing it. We are to shift the focus of our awareness from the doer to the deed. We do whatever tasks can bring us into union with God's own self-giving to the world: "We are coworkers with God" (2 Cor. 6:1, RCM).

THE MIND OF CAESAR

Among the pagans of Jesus' time, just the opposite principle was true. Gaining glory for oneself first—becoming a "Great One"—constituted the ideal of ancient society. Some people were believed to be born under a lucky star (astrological charts for newborns were a must, scrutinized for signs of destiny) or be favored by a divinity, as Julius Caesar was by Venus. Such specially gifted people had a destiny to fulfill and had a perfect right to expect other people's help in fulfilling it. Caesar loved, praised, and rewarded his soldiers in part because they willingly risked themselves for the glory of his destiny. Roman society especially prized the display of one's glory with appropriate qualities of "gravity" and "dignity."

People from elite families who were not descended from Venus or megaheroes like Caesar could embark on the course of "greatness" by following the *cursus honorum* or "way of honors." A series of short-term civic positions, ascending from sewer manager to consul or chief magistrate, could assure a person a respected position in society. Individuals spent enormous sums of money to promote their own name and cause, putting up plaques, funding public events like the theater or gladiatorial games, making lavish public sacrifices and ceremonies, and giving gifts to people who could help them advance socially.[1] Jesus called the version of such social climbing practiced in his native Israel "blowing a trumpet before you" while giving alms or doing some other good deed. (See Matt. 6:2.)

The organization of ancient urban society swirled around these "great ones." Lesser people vied to become the "clients" of such people and families, doing service and thus coming under their protection and the power of their influence. Traditional Christian baptismal liturgies labeled this "way of honor" as "the vain pomp and glory of the world,"[2] and the New Testament calls it "the pride of life" (1 John 2:16, KJV). The first part of the day for an important Roman might well be occupied in seeing a succession of client-petitioners who asked a favor in return for their promise to do anything the great one might request in the future. We see the last vestiges of this ancient social system in the so-called Mafia families with their godfather, or *capo,* and their pattern of offering protection to people and businesses in return for devotion and service.[3] Indeed, in one form or another, this organization around the great ones occurs in every society.

This perennial reality was impressed on me during my college years, when, for a while, I became just like an ancient Roman client to two powerful people in my hometown. As a working-class college kid during the recession that hit Detroit, Michigan, in 1960, I was having a difficult time finding a summer job that would pay enough to cover my share of college expenses for the coming year. But this working-class kid had received a scholarship to Yale University, so I phoned good old Charlie, the college recruiter who had visited my high school, encouraged us working-class kids to apply to his alma mater, and taken a shine to us. The next day I sat in his well-appointed office in a wealthy suburb while he made one phone call to the president of a major department store, also a Yale graduate. Within two hours, I found myself seated in the president's office chatting amiably about his college days and then headed to personnel to be processed for a summer job. After the three weeks of futile job searching, including an unsuccessful stab at that very department store, my head swam with awe at my first taste of what the right connections could do. I'm still very grateful to these men for using their power to help me, just as Yale at that point in its history was reaching out beyond its old, moneyed circles to include a richer diversity of students. But I am also well aware that without my status-enhancing admission to Yale, that help might not have been forthcoming. I had become part of an "old boy" network, one of the most influential and persistent forms of human organization. The danger is always that the old boys will help only other old boys.

THE BIBLE'S ALTERNATIVE VISION

According to Jesus, the vocation of the old boys is to help as many people as they can. Jesus' call to show greatness in servanthood stands in stark contrast to the ideals of the ancient pagan world. His teaching has roots in the Hebrew prophets who envisioned a culture of reciprocity in which the "least" are helped by "the greatest." In a society where the great ones had the power to orient society around themselves, the prophets aimed to counterbalance that orientation. They proclaimed that everyone is called to orient life around the service of God, who wishes all to have abundant life. Wealth, for example, is to be used not only for personal benefit but also for the less fortunate, "that there be no grinding poverty" among the poor who will always be a part of any society (see Deut. 15:11; Amos 6:4-7). Greatness comes from obedience to God:

> Their descendants will be mighty in the land;
> . . . .
> they are gracious, merciful, and righteous.
> It is well with those who deal generously and lend
> . . . .
> They have distributed freely, they have given to the poor;
> their righteousness endures forever.
> —Psalm 112:2, 4, 5, 9

Jesus roots his teaching about the power of money in these values. His tale of the wealthy man with bumper crops does not condemn wealth or disparage high crop yields. But rather than using the bumper crops to help the poor, the man builds bigger barns to hoard it all for himself. He is not "rich toward God" (see Luke 12:15-21). Practicing charity, for both Jesus and Jewish tradition,[4] is laying up "treasure in heaven" (see Luke 18:22). For Jesus, as for the prophets, money's significance lies in relationship among people and the good that money can do for the less fortunate in the community.

Such values seem hopelessly idealistic only to the short-sighted. If the wealthy do not invest in the fabric of society, they decrease their own safety in the long run through the rise of crime, class resentment, and eventually revolution. "Lend, expecting nothing in return," Jesus says, calling the "haves" to help the "have nots" better their lot (see Luke 6:35). In other words, in our day, invest your money in people-development, like the wealthy couple who sustains the boy choir of an inner-city church, the millionaire who funds scholarships for an entire inner-city school, or those of lesser means who tithe faithfully to causes that make a better world.[5]

But Jesus' vision goes further than this social pragmatism. He is talking about a conversion of the heart, a reorientation of the soul around a new center: the active, loving grace of God that wants to move through us for the sake of the world. Jesus issues a call to "sell all that you own," and "follow" the movement of that loving grace (Luke 18:22). Even in the New Testament, this call does not mean that we give away all our possessions. Mary and Martha, among others, clearly own property and have possessions. We are called, finally, to surrender everything we are and have into what one friend calls a "joint bank account with God." "So long as we can imagine the God of Jesus and the prophets cosigning every check, we're on the right track," he says.

In this sweeping vision, the truly great are those who lend their hearts, hands, and material resources to God's own passionate concern for justice, the setting right of all that is imbalanced and unjust in society and creation. God challenges the "great ones" of society to serve the common good. The great ones consecrate everything they have—money, prestige, power, influence—to God's purposes. Their model is Christ, who "though he was rich, . . . became poor" (2 Cor. 8:9). Jesus did not "grasp" at the great power and privilege of divinity but rather let that divine fullness take the form of a servant (see Phil. 2:6, NIV). So whatever fills us with power is to be yielded in service. This, Jesus said, is the way to greatness.

A HARD SELL

So great is the power of the "mind of Caesar" in us that this call of yielded service is a hard sell. I once facilitated a day of spiritual renewal for a highly dedicated group of people who worked for a local service organization that delivered meals to the elderly, drove the infirm to doctors, and offered other community support. I spent the first part of the morning talking about the model of Christ the Servant only to discover in the discussion that followed that these good folk were most uncomfortable with the idea that they might be considered servants.

Why, then, I asked, were they doing this? "Because I find it rewarding," replied one. "Personally fulfilling," commented another. "It's meaningful to help others, and it makes me feel good about myself," added yet another. "I'm uncomfortable thinking that what I do is service," said another man. "That seems to put me in a menial position, at the beck and call of another person."

Many people nowadays talk about service to the community in terms of personal self-fulfillment. While finding pleasure in doing good for others is both desirable and genuine, it is socially dangerous for that to be the only articulated reason. The shift from an older, religiously based ethic of "we all have to do our part" or "give back something" to "I find it really rewarding" is a shift away from the prophetic consciousness of reciprocity.

The people in my workshop were doing wonderful work; their actions were admirable, and their pleasure in it a great asset to their work. I thought highly of them and still do. They were using their superior resources to help those less fortunate than themselves. We might say they had taken step one toward Jesus' call: Use what you have to benefit others.

But these individuals' balking at "servanthood" revealed that the basis of their actions still contained strong elements of the mind of Caesar. Their deeds for others, in fact, subtly reinforced their sense of being "one-up" in the human pecking order. Their effort was praiseworthy as far as it went. In terms of the radical reorientation of soul that Jesus points to, it was just the first step.

SERVING THE TASK

There is a way beyond this subtle status orientation: serving the task. When we can enter fully into the task itself and let the doing itself become the center of our awareness, we are oriented away from the ego's status ruminations toward the goodness of the action itself and the reality of those it serves.

A natural self-forgetfulness characterizes what psychologists call "flow," in which we become so involved in an event that everything else becomes peripheral. Being caught up in a good task, one of the great joys of human life, offers a doorway out of the cramped preoccupations of the constantly plotting, scheming self. Along with contemplative meditation and deeply felt love, this portal to the connective state of mind is discussed in chapter 2. This phenomenon of self-forgetfulness, or flow, is encouraged by the Christian monastic practice of doing work in a centered, focused, "recollected" state of mind. Other parallels exist in the Buddhist work-practice of focusing awareness wholly on what one is doing without attachment to outcome and the Hindu practice of karma yoga, in which heart, mind, and body are trained to be involved fully in serving the task.

In the depths of the mind of Christ, our place in the pecking order ceases to be an operative part of consciousness. Rather, whatever will create, repair, and redeem the world becomes uppermost. We can cultivate such an attitude regularly by doing routine tasks mindfully, that is, putting our entire attention into the action rather than thinking about other things at the same time. This frame of mind connects us directly with the quality of the deed itself and the person or purpose for which we do it. Being so connected, we are likely to find ourselves called into deeper relationship, attentive to *whatever next needs to be done*. Ordinary actions become the training ground for more important deeds of service. Offering ourselves to be part of God's extension of love into the world can become a living reality.

A few years ago I noticed a visible increase in the volume of litter on the street in the pleasant suburban neighborhood where we live. Bottles and cans piled up near the stoplight at the corner; more papers seemed to find their way out of the hands of kids on the way home from school. Initially I reacted by fuming with annoyance as I picked up trash left on my property.

Then I observed that every few days, a well-dressed older man walked his dog through our neighborhood carrying a large paper bag. As he went along the street, he picked up trash wherever he found it—on everybody's property. To this day I don't know who he was, just what he did.

The man's action challenged and shamed me. What had blocked me from taking this obvious action myself? I walked my dog every day. I saw that trash. Yet all I could do was fume about slovenly people and fret over declining standards. He had, by contrast, taken upon himself an essentially menial task. Clearly a retired and affluent executive type, he was still not above cleaning the streets. I started carrying a bag myself as I walked the dog.

For whatever reason, the litter epidemic subsided, but I have never forgotten that man's example. Something needed to be done, and he did it, apparently just because it needed to be done. He "served the task" without concern for recognition or reward; he became the quiet servant of the neighborhood.

An old Asian tale contrasts three kinds of individuals: One does a good deed because she is with someone and wants to be thought a good person; one is among strangers but does the deed because she wishes to present a good face to them; and one is totally alone but does a deed like picking up trash simply because it is there to do.[6]

STRUGGLING COMPASSIONATELY

Dealing with our pecking-order tendencies is a process of continual conversion. We can handle the background muttering of our ego-driven status needs best in a gentle and compassionate fashion rather than in a brutal way. Like a child discovering a larger and more exciting world than her own backyard, the ego can be led to discover that some of life's deepest satisfactions, including the ego needs of feeling worthwhile and recognized, come from giving oneself to the task at hand.

Recently the good effect of focusing on the task was dramatized by a friend's experience in community service. The man I'll call Jim agreed to serve on the board of an agency specializing in assistance to AIDS sufferers. He was asked to take over as chair of the funding committee, which orchestrated an annual charity auction. His predecessor in this role, whom I'll call George, had tried to "help" the organization by using his considerable social weight and prestige to bring people and money to the event. While this approach had led to some success, the fallout from this leadership style was considerable. Committee members were faulted for not bringing in enough money and friends, and those on the committee who had less money and connections were simply ignored. Worst of all, the larger purpose of the funding committee—devising an overall strategy for diversifying fundraising—was being neglected. George sincerely wanted to be known as someone doing good in the community, and the auction provided his vehicle.

When Jim was asked to take over as chair of the auction committee, he made a vow to help the committee function in a different way. "I simply wanted the committee to fulfill its assigned purpose," he told me. He didn't have either George's social clout or money. But he was "greater" in people skills. He personally solicited the involvement of new and old members and invited fresh envisioning about how the agency could promote itself and diversify its funding. "For the first time, people began to get excited about the event," he said. Their excitement led them naturally to invite their friends to come to the carnival and to tap them for other gifts and services to the agency.

As this change in committee culture evolved, Jim steadfastly refused to take a public role at the auction, feeling that those immediately responsible should receive the credit—even though his status as committee chair made it appropriate for him to take credit. "That would just undermine what I'm trying to do in terms of people's ownership of the process," he said.

Just as George's efforts were not wholly selfish, Jim's altruism was not a pure and steady flame of noble self-sacrifice. It isn't that he wasn't looking for some reward. He certainly cared about whether people thought he was doing a good job; he wanted to be liked and considered useful. Declining the public recognition at the carnival "caused a bit of an inner twinge," he admitted. "Part of me said, 'Are you crazy?' and I wrestled with it a bit. But getting this committee to fulfill its purpose is more important than kudos for me. That's the reward I'm looking for."

And that's the reward that came. The committee flourished, and even George's talents, connections, and influence found their place in a scheme now larger than one man's efforts.

We've all "got it" in some way or another. Money, status, and social clout are only a few means to becoming "great ones." Some individuals offer great people skills, others offer humor, still others offer insight, while yet others excel in patience and endurance. In the light of Jesus' call for the "greatest" to be the "servants of all," the question is how that greatness will be used and to what ends.

The direction in which greatness mobilizes its energy, power, and resources can create great evil or great good. Cultivating the servant mind of Christ—dedication to the deed, not the doer—is a necessary element for staying in service to the good, especially when we confront evil. It is all too easy for those who side with the good to become enchanted by their own sense of moral superiority when faced with manifest evil, rather than humbly joining God's patient work to "overcome evil with good" (Rom. 12:21).

CHAPTER 14

Facing Evil

The Temptation of Malign Will

In the deep hours of the night, I awaken in a cold sweat from a nightmare:

We are watching a melodramatic enactment of a scene of horror. In a cold underground cave, on an ice floe in a chilly stream, a Frankenstein-like monster is menacing a supine lady. Like a shift in camera-angle, the view changes to include the audience area, almost empty except for a colleague and his wife and my wife and me. Is the horror only a performance after all? But then I become aware that somewhere behind us there is an even colder and more ominous presence. Something sinister is really at work here. The melodrama both conceals and contains it.

As I lie in bed calming myself down, I am still chilled even in the warm spring night. Some nightmares are obscure; this one is not. As a clergyman I'm dealing with an intensifying conflict between the colleague in my dream and a task force responsible for assisting him as a church administrator. At dinner the night before, my colleague and I discussed this increasingly impacted situation and vented our frustrations about it.

At one level, this human situation is ordinary—a difference over strategies. It has taken a somewhat byzantine turn, with clandestine conversations and unattractive power plays. What should have been a process of Christian conversation and civilized negotiation has come down, for the moment, to a contest of wills. The way of Caesar—power seeking, intimidation, pride, honor, and status—drives people in anger toward rash actions.

In and of itself, conflict is not evil. People differ and differences need to be settled somehow. Realistic solutions must "render to Caesar" due respect for pride, honor, status, and power-drive. But such conflict easily gives rise to something more, the danger of which the nightmare declares. That something more dwells in the cold rage I take to bed with me, my growing sense of righteous vindictiveness, and my livid images characterizing other people's behavior as "monstrous." In truth, everyone in the conflict thinks everyone else is monstrous. They are all probably seething in the same way I am.

Part of me says this behavior is all pretty melodramatic—a tempest in a teapot. Surely the "monster" aspect to this situation is just a product of our overheated imaginations, our psychological projections. But the second part of the dream—when it becomes nightmarish—alerts me to the fact that a real monster lurks in this situation, and it's not the one "onstage" in the outer conflict's melodrama. It's behind us—behind me!—insinuating its cold tentacles into the very pores of our souls. The danger does not lie in the outer drama, which surely could be handled through the offices of a good conflict-management consultant. The danger is, even now, working unseen inside us, in the cave of our hearts, luring us and tempting us toward what I have over the years come to call "malign willfulness"—the determination to manipulate, distort, diminish, demean, and even destroy whatever stands in the way of one's own dreams, visions, and desires. In the simplest terms, it's "up to no good."

FIGHTING EVIL WITH EVIL?

If we're up to no good—aggressive, hostile, overtly selfish—the destructiveness of our intentions becomes visible to all, and we are more likely to get called to accountability. When we see ourselves as righteous combatants in a good cause, we are most likely to remain unconscious of the darker side of our desires. We are most vulnerable to malign intent in our own hearts when we are up against real evil in the world—"cosmic powers of this present darkness" that block God's desires for good in the world (Eph. 6:12).[1]

The danger surfaces when we identify our own will with the Right Thing. This identification leads to justification of getting our own way, whatever the cost, because we're getting rid of evil. Thus malign willfulness can hide itself cleverly, like a computer virus, behind all sorts of noble guises: righteousness, victimhood, and even a fervent identification with God's will. Our very desire to destroy the evil may lead us to be "overcome by evil" and commit evil ourselves (see Rom. 12:21).

Thus, in responding to evil, we often perpetrate evil individually or corporately—sometimes in vengeful retaliation, like the firebombing of Dresden in World War II as a payback for the London Blitz. Sometimes it is "preventive," like dropping the atom bombs on Hiroshima and Nagasaki as a warning to the Japanese, producing a holocaust of hundreds of thousands of sacrificial victims. Sometimes it is purgative, like a lynching or capital execution for a particularly heinous crime, making many feel the world has been "cleansed" of evil. On a personal level we may seek to upbraid, lecture, shame, or intimidate wrongdoers, zing them with sarcasm, or trounce them in argument.

We can debate at great length whether evil springs from an ultimate source like Satan without being able to prove anything one way or another. But human experience presents evidence of the power of malign willfulness again and again. Even if our disagreements begin for legitimate reasons, we are always in danger of the sinister presence "behind us," an entire way of thinking, feeling, imagining, and acting that sets us on the path of perpetrating evil consciously or unconsciously.

I should have been on high alert for my own righteous rage long before the nightmare, since I had been fuming about the unintended injury inflicted on people by this task force's procedures for many years. For my outspokenness, I have now been appointed to be part of the very process I have abhorred.

I'm certainly going to work to make the procedures more graceful, just, and humane. But the sinister force lurking behind me, in my own soul, is a warning that I dare not be a righteous crusader. My convictions may be on the side of the angels, but if my spirit is not aligned with God's Spirit, my presence and actions will only add to the evil.

All the psychological power of the pecking order we explored in the previous chapter comes to the aid of the righteous crusader. Such crusaders need to be in control to stop evil. They must have power over bad people and bad things to prevent their getting out of hand. They definitely consider themselves one up in the pecking order because they're on the side of the good, and those other people have lower status because they're supporting evil or are evil. Being a righteous crusader can be a real thrill.

None of this posturing, of course, is the way of Christ, which is intended to "overcome evil with good" (Rom. 12:21). The way of Christ begins in alertness to the dark potentials of our own hearts and aims always to maximize the good in any situation. It relies on the immediate availability of grace more than the flexing of Caesar's muscles.

THE HAZARDS OF HOLY HATRED

Christ's way often has not been the way of Christians. Christians, along with Muslims and Jews, the other heirs of the biblical tradition, are especially vulnerable to what I call "holy hatred." The Bible reveals a God passionately on the side of good, offering a dazzling dream of a world "where righteousness is at home" (2 Pet. 3:13). This God does not exist beyond good and evil like the Supreme Self of Eastern religion. We are called to take sides in a struggle against all that hinders God's grace from flowing freely through human hearts and actions. We are invited to pray daily for God's desires to be done "on earth as . . . in heaven." At the same time, however, we are warned that we must pray to be delivered from evil, perhaps because Jesus realized the danger inherent in the passions of the righteous crusader.

Jesus certainly could see that danger reflected in some of the psalms, where the cry of the good soul trapped by arrogant oppressors can easily boil over in bloodthirsty fury: "Do I not hate those who hate you, O Lord? . . . I hate them with perfect hatred; I count them my enemies" (Ps. 139:21-22). When fully aroused, this holy hatred leads to an inevitable conclusion: "The righteous will rejoice when they see vengeance done; they will bathe their feet in the blood of the wicked" (Ps. 58:10).

The prayerfully pondered, religion-fueled terrorist attacks on the World Trade Center were horrific examples of how the violent side of this biblical heritage can lead people astray when it is taken out of context and not balanced by the revelation of God's *merciful* justice. Jesus' teachings as well as Jewish and Muslim traditions clearly hold up that mercy. All three traditions emphasize that God, even in justified wrath over evil, remembers mercy (Hab. 3:2, a prayer based on the conviction that God is merciful) in strategizing a response. We are called to do the same. (For a full discussion of this theme, see chapter 8.)

The call to mercy means that even if we feel called to go to battle in a cause we deem just, standards of conduct still apply. In a telling scene from the film *Band of Brothers*, an American paratrooper in the Normandy invasion of 1944 discovers that a captured German soldier grew up in the same town in the United States where he did. The German soldier's parents had returned to "aid the Fatherland," and the boy ended up in the German army. The two soldiers fall into animated discussion about familiar neighborhoods and neighbors, their common humanity asserting itself over the chasm of their differences. The paratrooper's sergeant is quite annoyed at this outbreak of fellow feeling in the midst of battle. "Stop fraternizing with the enemy," he insists with increasing anger. When the paratrooper leaves, the sergeant takes out his gun and executes the German prisoners in cold blood. Unable to remember mercy, he knowingly breaks the rules of war designed to remember the humanity of the enemy even on the battlefield.

Jesus could see such vengeful fury all around him in his own day, some of it expressed in dark apocalyptic dreams of vengeance like those that found their way into the Christian book of Revelation in the New Testament, which depicts a cosmic bloodbath to rid the world once and forever of evil. In the face of such vengefulness, his call to "bless those who curse you" (Luke 6:28) is truly remarkable and becomes a mandate for our actions that permanently challenges our bloodthirsty instincts.

HUMBLE AWARENESS OF SHADOW AND "SPRAY EFFECT"

The anger in these violent texts does not make them problematic. Such anger is a natural *first* reaction to injustice. There would be something wrong with us if we did not become initially angry when encountering evil. But what do we do after that initial burst of anger? In light of the call to "remember mercy" even in the midst of wrath, these texts give us the first clue to maintaining a stance of creative, constructive love in the face of the world's evil, for they invite us to become fully conscious of our rage against evil. We dare not lose track of the rage, for it can so easily lead us into evil.

The dream about the monsters in the cave issued a grace-filled wake-up call. Prior to the dream, all I could see was my righteous rage at what I considered wrong. I had responded to the first few task-force meetings with a combination of heartsickness and hot, smoldering anger that shot my blood pressure up to dangerous levels. These well-meaning people, in my view, were not sufficiently aware of the sinister "shadow" side of their behavior. Being nice folk, they were uncomfortable facing the full destructive effect of their actions on other people's lives.

The dream jolted and humbled me, warning me of the evil that could emerge from me if I stayed unconscious of my own sinister, shadow side. My righteous fury had been "seen" by the dream. Now I could take a more dispassionate look at myself and the others involved in the situation. Those pursuing policies I do not favor are imperfect, flawed human beings, just like me, pursuing the good as they see it. I am called to reach out to the good in them, not curse them.

Crusaders too often remain blissfully unaware of the ambiguities involved in human situations, making easy contrasts between good and evil, light and darkness, right and wrong in order to mobilize human passions. A friend of mine who participated in the 1963 civil rights march on Washington spent the day thrilled by the speeches of Martin Luther King Jr. and other civil rights leaders. The hundreds of thousands of like-minded folk filling the Mall and momentum of the movement exhilarated him. He spent much of that night at a vigil at the Lincoln Memorial feeling buoyed by his participation in the forward thrust of history. Then, in the early morning hours, he had a dream in which he was handing a shotgun to George Wallace, the outspoken, racist governor of Alabama! He awoke, deeply troubled by the realization that his own actions for the good might, in fact, directly provoke destructive response. He also awakened from of his own social naïveté, for he saw that in the usual pattern, he could expect oppression to intensify when challenged.

The late Lawrence Rose, my seminary dean, characterized that kind of unwanted outcome as the "spray effect." Any action, no matter how good, Dean Rose taught, may have an unintended evil consequence. For that reason, he said, we are unwise to be smug and self-confident even in the pursuit of the good. Rather, we should be alert and alive to unintended consequences. We cannot imagine our actions existing in some protected, pure sphere. Every deed enters into a web of uncontrollable interconnections and consequences, and no one remains entirely exempt from causing evil consequences. Supporting economic sanctions against South Africa to protest apartheid, Iraq to protest militaristic dictatorship, or the Ivory Coast to protest slave labor may cause suffering among ordinary citizens already oppressed by unjust regimes. We may very well choose to take such actions—divesting in a company or boycotting a product—but in so doing we are called to forgo the rewarding thrill of righteousness and the accompanying delusion that we are untainted by evil. Our good action may cause suffering for others. We are enmeshed in the suffering and evil of the world and cannot stand outside of it. If we choose such an action, we hope to do more good than evil.

ACTIVE INTERCESSION AND LIVELY EXPECTANCY

Such actions need to be taken in a spirit of active, expectant prayer. Just like "marinating" one's stubbed toe or pained back in the atmosphere of blessing, all the evil-dominated situations that attract our concern need to be actively placed in the larger sphere of Spirit rather than being held tightly in the overheated cauldron of our own isolated minds.

Jesus comes to us in "the power of the Spirit" (Luke 4:14) so that we do not have to face the "principalities and powers" with our own unaided strength. Saint Paul urges us to "be strong in the Lord and in the strength of his power. . . . Pray in the Spirit at all times in every prayer and supplication" (Eph. 6:10, 18). This is not a matter of getting God on our side but rather of letting our psyche be influenced by God. We are not simply to offer special prayers for a situation but "at all times" to cultivate a different mind and heart about it.

Each time the memory of a difficult situation comes into my consciousness, I can offer the situation to God. Each time my mind charges off in a furious review of possible actions, I can open myself to the illumination of the Spirit. My fretting, stewing, pondering, plotting, and planning are more and more suffused with an active openness to God, a willing release of this situation to God's actions through me and beyond me. Instead of the pure witness against evil, I realize that I myself collude in ways known and unknown with the world's evil. Instead of the righteous crusader, I seek merely to be a flawed vessel of love.

After the nightmare, I participated in the next meeting of the task force quite differently, internally at least. As I drove to the meeting, I put myself in a state of meditative prayer, cultivating an inner state of receptivity to the Spirit. As I greeted people, I intentionally blessed them with the light and love of God. As the meeting began, I inwardly offered it to God's good purposes and held that intention steadily as the group's reactivity to the latest round of conflict with my colleague escalated. Rather than sitting back and stewing about what to say, I kept my bright, clever, and righteous opinions to myself and sought to speak only when I felt a gentle urging from deep within.

But most importantly, *I surrendered the whole process of this conflict to the Spirit's working.* That surrender is at the heart of intercession: we actively pour out our concerns, placing them in the flow of God's goodness; then we let go of the outcome. Rather than seeking to manipulate the process in any way, I could participate when moved to do so, be silent when provoked to unhelpful wrath, and expectantly await what good might emerge. I sat there that evening in a state of active, expectant, prayerful *yearning* for God's good action among us. As of this writing, the situation continues to work itself out, but that active, expectant yearning continues to be the heart space into which I place all my fretting and worrying about the task force.

My task force difficulties don't even begin to approach coming up against the great principalities and powers that cause evil and havoc in the world. The task force is a group of reasonably well-intentioned people in conflict. But the "monster behind us" lurks in every human conflict, ready to emerge. Every situation like this, no matter how minor, offers a chance to practice facing evil, actual or merely suspected, with charity and prayer for the good rather than hating and despising the evil. As a wise old woman once said to me, "The devil fears nothing more than the milk of human kindness"—that and hearts that sincerely want to seek, find, and serve the good.

How such practice in small matters might lead one to spiritual capacities with which to face great evil is given dramatic expression in *War in Heaven,* one of the mystical novels by Charles Williams. A saintly Anglican archdeacon combats genuinely diabolical forces of evil working through a practitioner of black magic. Seeking to confront this evil, which is out to destroy the life of an innocent young boy, the archdeacon finds himself delivered into its hands, as have so many prophets, martyrs, and ordinary folk who have stood against evil through the ages. Instead of fighting the evil forces with hatred, he surrenders himself inwardly to the divine Goodness that "caught and returned upon them the energies they had put forth."[2] In a simple and wholehearted way, he returned good for evil.

Such a practice can have great power in difficult situations. Evil wants us to be afraid, reactive, and hostile, drawing us subtly to its side. In the days following the World Trade Center attacks, I heard an interview with an Egyptian who had been terrorized by four young men when they vandalized his coffee shop late one night. The police, alert to anti-Arab hate crimes, had caught the young men within the hour and returned them to the restaurant for identification. The owner identified them but declined to press charges, saying he would prefer to forgive rather than retaliate. An hour later, the young men showed up again—to apologize and offer restitution. The owner's action had made these self-righteous thugs realize that all Arabs weren't evil. He made them coffee, and they sat with a group of Arab men until dawn, talking about common fears and feelings.

Actual rejoicing

The archdeacon in Williams's story prepared himself for a prayerful encounter with evil by the habitual practice of praise. Phrases from Psalm 136, such as, "O give thanks unto the God of gods, for his mercy endureth forever" (KJV), are constantly on his lips, especially when facing opposition of any kind. The Way of Christ invites us even more radically to "rejoice" when we face any difficulty, including confrontation with entrenched forces of opposition to the Kingdom: "Whenever you face trials of any kind, consider it nothing but joy" (James 1:2).

A particular strand of conservative, charismatic Christian piety advocates immediate thanksgiving over any occurrence, however tragic or evil it may be. When I first heard this idea, I considered it dangerous at best, seriously demented at worst. I still consider it potentially dangerous if used to bury feelings of outrage, hurt, or grief. But gradually I have come to see this practice as part of the counterintuitive logic of the gospel pathway.

A man who struggled with his wife's alcoholism set me on the road to this realization some years ago by grouping the words of institution in the Eucharist in a different way. One night after services he came to me with a bemused look on his face and said, "I've never noticed this, but tonight I heard it this way: 'In the night in which he was betrayed, he gave thanks. . . .'[3] Isn't that an odd response to betrayal? What does it mean?"

What indeed? I pondered then. Over the years I've slowly pondered my way toward praise. My regular practice of responding to frustration with blessing has helped me to this seemingly crazy wisdom as an emotionally honest practice. With enough experience, one can begin to see that, as an old Portuguese proverb has it, "God writes straight with crooked lines." If we're facing difficulty, opposition, or real evil with active intercession, committing it to the mysterious working of grace and actively anticipating the surprising ways that good may appear, then why not begin to give thanks for that good now?

In biblical prayer, the heartrending psalms of lament most often begin with an outpouring of difficulty and distress, move through impassioned pleas for divine assistance, and conclude with praise. As Eugene Peterson says of the Psalms, "Any prayer, no matter how desperate its origin, no matter how angry and fearful the experiences it traverses, ends up in praise."[4] At least that is the expectant hope of the believing heart, and thus the reason to cultivate a sense of rejoicing at the beginning of difficulties: "Though I walk through the valley of the shadow of death, I will fear no evil" (Ps. 23:4, KJV).

I have a long track record of fretting over the ungodly (see Ps. 37:1-2). The word *fret* means, among other definitions, "to fray"—to unravel edges of fabric—an apt description of the harm we do to our own souls when we stew and fume and fuss and fear over what we consider evil. Evil's greatest power is intimidating us, hooking us on our own fears. Fear will lead directly to the reactivity that summons all the juices of anger, demonization of the other, and temptation to do evil to protect ourselves or destroy the threat. Biblical faith invites us to "trust in the LORD and do good" (Ps. 37:3). The advice is psychologically and strategically sound.

"I've really come to love it when the Opposition comes up to block something I feel called to do," declares my nurse-healer friend Nancy Orlen Weber. "First, it confirms for me I'm onto an important issue. Second, it's a challenge to get even smarter than the Opposition. The Opposition keeps you on your toes."

Outcomes belong to God, not to us. There's a great old Chinese tale about a farmer whose son captures a wonderful wild horse. The neighbor says, "Isn't that wonderful!" but the old man just says, "We shall see what comes of it." As the boy tries to tame the wild horse, he is thrown and breaks a leg. The neighbor laments, "Isn't that terrible!" but the old man just says, "We shall see what comes of it." The Emperor's men come to the town and force all the young men—except the injured son—to go off and face death in the latest war. The neighbor rejoices, "Isn't it fortunate!" And the old man says, "We shall see what comes of it." For the Christian, what "comes of it" depends on the goodness of a God who, in all things, "works for good" (Rom. 8:28, RSV).

How do I know what possibilities for good lie hidden in my colleague's conflict with the task force? Who can foresee what the grace of God, working through countless hundreds or thousands, may bring out of any tragic event, evil policy, or act of evil?

Praise keeps our eyes open for the unpredictable, even when we face the darkness.

PART III

Offering the Self for Partnership

God wants us to live magnificently. "Offering the obstacles" of our nature for transformation helps us become more freely cooperative with God's purposes for the world. We are created to be the mediators of God's own justice, love, wisdom, and creativity in all our relationships: to self, to others, and to the world.

We are "earthlings," created by God to do earthly things in heavenly ways, as the guardian species of this planet's life.[1] Human beings have a few fundamental tasks in this world, according to the story of our origins in Scripture.[2] We are here to learn

- how to live in love and justice with one another;
- how to "tend and keep" the earth, responsibly relating to all its creatures;
- and how to prayerfully breathe in God's own desires for those relationships.

The spirit in which we do these tasks can make of our relationships at home, at work, or in the community either a paradise or a purgatory. The values and attitudes we bring to crafting the landscape, harvesting natural resources, and dealing with other species either enrich or devastate the earth. Most of life's rough edges appear when people are engaged in these fundamental tasks.

177

According to Saint Paul's staggeringly beautiful vision, earth itself yearns for us to take up these tasks, waiting "with eager longing for the revealing of the children of God" (Rom. 8:19). The world and all its creatures are looking for human beings strong and wise enough to "tend and keep" life here on earth well, human beings who find their deepest joy in following the Creator's dreams for the development of this world. Humanity too, whether knowingly or not, yearns for Messiah, the "desire of nations," to come. The visions of the sages and prophets in Scripture outline that dream: a world "where righteousness dwells" (2 Pet. 3:13, KJV paraphrase) where the "trees of the forest shall sing for joy" (see Isa. 55:12; Ps. 96:12), and the nations of the world will not "learn war any more" (Mic. 4:3, KJV).

Human beings are meant to be the chief earthly enactors of that dream, which accords with our own deepest needs and desires. We are to do the things that our species is gifted to do—farming and crafting, eating and drinking, loving and learning, taking the stuff of earth and transforming it—in a very particular spirit: loving-kindness, justice, and humility (see Mic. 6:8). The next chapters will explore taking up each of these tasks in that graceful state of mind.

CHAPTER 15

Befriending the Soul in Self and Others

We don't decide who we are. We discover who we are and decide what to do about it. For those who do not settle for an idealized, self-avoiding image of themselves, life is peppered with ongoing revelations about the real quality of their souls—hopes, dreams, desires, and capacities that sometimes come as a surprise.

As I sat on the floor of my dormitory room with catalogs spread out before me in the spring of my sophomore year in college, trying to decide on a major, a voice within me kept saying "biology"! I had made myself prayerfully receptive to an inner play of feelings and ideas because I couldn't make up my mind between history and English as my major. I had been a history buff since early childhood, catching my grandmother's romantic love of ancient sagas and old-fashioned ways. History was in my blood and would be an easy major. English Literature offered new horizons and a chance to hone writing skills that would be important in my chosen profession, the ministry, but it would require a lot of hard work. Nonetheless, there was "biology!" pounding in the back of my brain like an unexpected guest.

Biology? I said, half to myself and half to God. *What sense does that make? It has nothing to do with the ministry. I did enjoy my freshman biology class, but I've never been all that interested in the sciences. Where's this coming from?*

I chose the easy path and majored in history. It wasn't until my third year in ordained ministry that I realized why "biology!" had come knocking on the door of my conscious mind. By that time, I had become very interested in natural theology—the study of nature and human nature for signs of divine Presence and creativity. The writings of Pierre Teilhard de Chardin on biological evolution as the emergence of consciousness intrigued me, and his experience of nature as part of "the divine milieu" had drawn me deeper into the natural world. I was in the middle of reading a book on DNA by Isaac Asimov in preparation for a sermon series on science and religion when the obvious finally dawned: "Omigod," I blurted out. "I should have majored in biology."

I really don't know whether God urged me to major in biology during that sophomore quandary or something in me knew better than my conscious mind what I really wanted. In either case, on that pivotal night, I declined to dialogue with a God-given aspect of myself that had something to offer in service to God. I reacted with suspicion, distrust, and dismissal to the notion.

I had been well trained in the art of self-dismissal. People of my generation were taught not to "pay too much attention to yourself" from earliest childhood. Any expression of delight in or love of self was especially frowned on. As a friend puts it, "My mama told me not to go around dwelling on my good points!" Alas, Mama no doubt did and most likely Daddy too, if they had listened to the local preacher. Yet while the Scripture bids us not to "think of yourselves more highly than you ought to think" (Rom. 12:3), it does not bid us to ignore ourselves entirely! Jesus himself invites us to a healthy, self-accepting love of ourselves.

THE SELF AS OTHER

Jesus also makes it clear that self-love and love for others connect intimately when he says, "Love your neighbor as yourself" (Matt. 22:39). From the first moment of conscious life, self and other are mysteriously joined. One of the first "others" we meet in life is our own mysterious self as we explore our body, and our abilities unfold. The mysterious self is not just one entity. We are all a rather ramshackle collection of diverse, sometimes competing aspects, made up of urges and yearnings, impulses and abilities, desires and dreams, operating mostly in the dark of the unconscious mind. One by one, they present themselves to our consciousness in response to new life situations, knocking at the door until they are acknowledged and dealt with.

We observe this unfolding clearly as innate abilities emerge in the first few years of a child's incredible development and growth. A healthy and holy self-love begins, in part, with the healthy narcissism of our earliest childhood—the delighted pleasure a child takes in her awakening skills, discovering that she is "fearfully and wonderfully made" (Ps. 139:14).

My two-and-a-half-year-old nephew, Elias, full of delight in his amazing God-given brain and body, was sitting politely at the dinner table one day, eating and talking as much like the grown-ups as he could manage. "Please pass the salt," he said slowly and deliberately. It was passed. "Thank you," he responded, and sprinkled some on his food. Then he blinked, and said in a soft, astonished voice, "I . . . did that . . . rather . . . *well!*"

And so he did! Elias's wide-eyed amazement at himself, that dawning sense of the self as a mysterious gift rather than prideful possession generates healthy self-love, wholesome humility, and ability to receive others with the same generous delight.

I once heard a sermon that used childhood stories like this to illustrate the power of original sin. "A young child is the most selfish creature on earth—always hungry, always demanding, then always asking you to notice what he or she is doing." I shuddered, realizing how much religious teaching has followed this line of thinking. That perspective subverts our learning all the ways the Divine can love and embrace us, not only through others but also through ourselves. Rather than disparage this stage of development, we need to embrace it as Jesus did the little children. Jesus' invitation to "love your neighbor as yourself" implies that we cultivate the same pleasurable response to the good aspects of ourselves that we would in any other person. In so doing, we actually are loving God, because the good quality we love in self or other is a reflection of the divine nature itself. That is why "those who do not love a brother or sister whom they have seen, cannot love God whom they have not seen" (1 John 4:20). Loving the good in ourselves strengthens our ability to love the good qualities at play in others. Jesus was a master at seeing these good parts of others. He could rejoice in the image of God at play in others because he knew the image of God at work in himself.

Saint Bernard would call this primary delight in oneself the first stage of growth in love: love of self for one's own sake.[1] At this level, one also loves others and even God for one's own sake: for what they can do for me. The world is centered around the emerging self. The underlying purr of this narcissistic self-delight continues to be a crucial foundation for later, more advanced stages of confidence, self-esteem, and the ability to offer one's self to others in service. According to Bernard, the goal is learning to love oneself and others for God's sake—to enter into God's own love for the world and all its creatures. Even in the first steps of self-centered love, we have begun to learn a skill central to God's love for us: recognizing and caring for whatever comes into view, then deciding how to deal with it in the most loving fashion.

Truly loving the self involves willingly befriending what emerges into the light of consciousness. Befriending doesn't mean always agreeing or cooperating. It means, in a way, treating the different aspects of ourselves as "others," the same way we might treat them if they appeared in other people. We listen respectfully, cooperate or resist as is appropriate, and cherish or forgive, as called for. Should some aspect of the self prove difficult or an enemy, we practice the difficult art of blessing it and praying for it, seeking out the heart of its disturbance, rather than hating it, cursing it, and seeking to destroy it—even while we restrain ourselves from acting it out. Only so can we fully allow the image of God in us to grow toward its mature fullness.

THE CONTINUAL SURPRISE OF SELF-DISCOVERY

"New occasions teach new duties," says the old hymn,[2] and new occasions sometimes evoke from us aspects of the self we didn't imagine were there. If we do not show hospitality to the strangers that arise from within, we may miss a call of God.

For one minister, aching wrists signaled a need to befriend an aspect of herself. Nearing midlife, Karen felt stalled in her spiritual growth and on the verge of serious depression and was plagued by incipient arthritis. As we explored some of the ways she had experienced a sense of sacredness in her early life, she remembered the love she once had for drawing.

Why had she given it up? In her family, drawing wasn't considered serious enough to waste time on, so she'd pursued it on the margins of her life. She'd tried to do some drawing in college but had fallen in with a crowd of serious companions who ridiculed her efforts. So she'd turned her attention to the matters she had been schooled to regard as truly important, eventually going into the ministry of the Word in a denomination that prized clear thinking and worthy social action.

As we talked, her wrists ached. Of course, it might be arthritis, but could this be the ache of heart and hands that wanted to draw? It took Karen a while to summon the courage to pick up a pencil, so deeply had she internalized the unloving rejection of her artistic self. When she finally did start to draw again, a cascade of images emerged. She moved into pastels. Her hands dug into fresh clay and shaped images of her own soul and then of the Holy. She loved what she was doing, and she loved herself doing it. The ache in her wrists disappeared. Even more importantly, she had welcomed and received an aspect of God's own image in herself, an expression of God's own artistry. Only so could she freely claim it for her own well-being and offer it for

God's purposes in the world. Art soon became a part of her ministry to others.

Karen had been carefully taught to subvert the divine love for her by rejecting the "unimportant" parts of herself. We may begin by accepting a quality within ourselves for our own happiness and well-being—"for our own sake," in Bernard's terms—but that very quality is linked, however obscurely, to a quality of the divine Being. Karen's talent quickly became available "for God's sake," through her own ministry. Loving and using a divine part of ourselves probably will lead us out of self-preoccupation to service, for any good quality comes from God and is a road to God.

LOVING THE DIFFICULT PARTS

The continuing process of self-discovery may present us with some unhappy surprises—immature parts of ourselves, distorted eruptions of the image of God, and even destructive impulses. Just as God makes the sun shine on the just and the unjust and rain to fall on the good and the wicked, we are called to compassionate treatment of the whole of our selves.

The need for compassion applies especially to the parts of ourselves that are genuinely difficult or dangerous. We discussed offering the obstacles in Part 2. But we can note an important additional practice. So closely aligned is the love of other parts of ourselves and the love of other people that we can get a clue on how to love the difficult parts of ourselves by practicing on people we find difficult. ("Love" here doesn't mean affectionate feelings but an active intention for the other person's well-being and an openness to see another with compassion.)

One evening, after a session on claiming our own experience of God, a participant cornered me with a list of not-so-subtly hostile questions. Why was I giving so much credit to people's experiences? Wasn't it my duty as a priest to tell people the truth rather than trust the ill-informed opinions of the mob? What was wrong with the church these days anyway? Why did they always want to change everything?

At first I felt simply put off. Warm and toasty from a smoothly running session in which most people had participated enthusiastically, the last thing I wanted was this squeaky wheel. But there I was, every inch the priest in full dark suit and collar, and I knew I needed to listen. So I breathed deeply, let go of my annoyance, and tuned in to the woman, listening not only to the words but to the feelings behind the words. On the surface I sensed the anger—cold, clear, well spoken, and deadly quiet. I wondered how nasty this would get. Behind the anger I began to catch the undercurrent of sadness. A person of deeply conservative convictions, this woman found herself in a church that had changed radically in a liberal direction. Church traditions precious to her had been derided and discarded. I began hearing the plaintive groan behind the cascade of complaints. As I heard that, my compassion was aroused, and I was able to begin telling her I could understand her distress over these losses. I finally glimpsed, behind her anger and sadness, a deep and unspoken hurt. Her church had betrayed something important to her spirituality.

I can't claim I did a very good job of mollifying her, much less helping her to a better frame of mind. But I did befriend her sadness and hurt. She knew she was really being listened to, not dismissed.

That experience led me to respond differently to myself the next time I heard myself bursting out in a torrent of cold, angry complaining. The image of that woman came up in my mind, and I heard her own voice in mine. That realization broke the stride of my abrasive complaint, and I began to wonder what the hurt behind my anger might be. Finding it, I could murmur "you poor thing" to myself by way of comfort, get a more accurate bead on my reasons for distress, and return to deal with people I had flared at with a calmer and clearer head.

We often dislike most vehemently the qualities in others that we are most afraid of in ourselves. Could it be that in the mystery of grace we are to learn something about ourselves from the difficult people who cross our paths? I am, for example, enormously annoyed by rudeness or lack of consideration. "How dare people act that way," I used to fume. And yet, truth be told, I am very haphazard in my consideration of other people. Seldom actively rude, I do not consistently deliver the ordinary niceties that make people feel they are being dealt with courteously. My "thank-you's" are spotty; I ask people to do things and do not sustain them with regular praise and support; and I sometimes get so enthusiastically caught up in what I'm doing that I don't pay sufficient attention to other people's agendas. So I have learned to use other people's rudeness as an occasion for reflection, not just on their behavior but on mine: *Oh, this is what it feels like to be treated that way . . . hmm; maybe they're just haphazard or preoccupied like me. . . . Nonetheless, please note for future reference: it doesn't feel good.*

With such ruminations we befriend a difficulty in a way that leads to genuine repentance and growth as well as enlarges our heart's capacity to bear with the faults sympathetically. This response does not preclude our deciding to challenge someone else's bad behavior. It makes it more likely, however, that our challenge will be clear and clean, not distorted by unconscious projection of our own faults on others.

The mystery of mutual indwelling

We see others in ourselves and ourselves in others all the time. What we call the "self" is, in fact, woven mysteriously out of elements drawn from other people as well as arising from within us. As small children we internalize emotional rhythms from the adults around us and begin to imitate people we admire, consciously or unconsciously. We develop crushes on teachers and admire other kids because we want to internalize a quality we love in them. Often we are drawn to a quality precisely because it exists in us already, yearning to be stimulated into growth. We are drawn to teachers, mentors, and friends in order to love them and enjoy what happens to us when we are with them.

I grew up at a great emotional distance from my sensuous, instinctual self and separated from awareness of my body, spending my teen years and early twenties virtually locked in my head, "about two inches behind my eyes," as I remember saying. In my senior year in seminary, a new student, whom I'll call Christian, arrived who embodied my lost instinctual self. He moved like a panther, lived through his feelings, and did everything with a joyful sensuousness. Not only was I drawn to him in friendship, but in his presence that lost part of me came alive. A sleek black panther started appearing in my dreams, radiant with new life. For a long while, I needed to be in touch with Christian to be in touch with that part of myself, but slowly I became able to evoke this God-rooted ability to love life with all my senses for myself. Still, the contact was tenuous. Once, in my first year of ordained ministry, I called Christian and begged him to visit precisely because I was losing touch with this new part of myself and needed his presence to reconnect.

For Christian, I carried the clarity of mind he desired. He has sought me out through the years when he wanted to think through a question clearly. In these matters, we have been, as Saint Paul put it, "members of one another" (Eph. 4:25).

Other aspects of people come to live in us. My wife's deep, sardonic humor has come to dwell in me over the years, lightening a soul too seriously engaged with the dark side of life to let go with a belly laugh. I shrug my shoulders, tilt my head, and hold up my hands in a gesture of "who knows?" just the way my Israeli friend Walter does. As I grow older, I find myself shaking my finger to make a point the way my grandfather did. We rub off on one another in profound ways.

Each self is a mixture of the many selves by which it has been touched. In modern culture, we sometimes feel such a desire to "be myself" that we try to exorcise traits we may have "copied" from another person. People express distress especially over similarities to parents or other childhood authorities. Discovering our mother's tone of voice or our father's way of handling money coming across the border from the unconscious alarms us. While we may seek to modify our behavior if these borrowed patterns are not helpful, we will not do it well by rejecting our inner mother or father. Only by blessing these inner parts of the self can we come to wholeness of life. By accepting them, we are freed to love others with our whole heart.

LOVING SELF AND OTHER IN PRAYER

The deepest level of befriending both self and other is prayer, for in prayer we learn to love ourselves and others "for God's sake," as Saint Bernard puts it. By prayer I do not mean an act of turning away from the world or others to God but rather *turning more deeply toward ourselves, others, and in the world IN God.*

In the reality of co-inherence, God, others, and I are distinct but not wholly separate. We are united as differing manifestations of the same qualities. As we come to know and claim this reality, we are delivered from the narrow hothouse of merely personalistic relationship and delivered into a deeper, transpersonal level in which we love, appreciate, and care for others not only for our own reasons but for God's. We become the stream of God's love for others, a stream made deeper and richer by intentional prayer.

As I consciously put myself into the flow of God's loving energies to the world, invoking a sense of God's all-pervasive presence, I can direct my attention to the "other," whether that be in my soul or in the world, as a channel of grace. Charles Williams describes such intercessory prayer in *The Greater Trumps.* Sybil, whose whole life is prayer, prays for her niece:

> She turned to her habitual resource. She emptied her
> mind of all thoughts and pictures: she held it empty till
> the sudden change in it gave her the consciousness of the
> spreading out of the stronger will within; then she
> allowed that now unimportant daily mind to bear the
> image and memory of Nancy into its presence. She did

not, in the ordinary sense, "pray for" Nancy; . . . she
merely held her own thought of Nancy stable in the midst
of Omniscience. [3]

The "image" of Nancy in Sybil's mind mysteriously connects
with Nancy herself. We are all part of the "bundle of the living"
(1 Sam. 25:29). All souls are interconnected in God.[4]

Faithfulness to this divine streaming of Love, which is the real
Source of all our inspirations to pray, requires befriending the
call to prayer when it comes, however perplexing it may be. Early
on in my practice of intercessory prayer, the image of a friend of
a friend, whom I'll call Leo, popped into my mind along with
the urge to pray for the young man, whom I hardly knew at all.
I held the image of Leo into God's light and prayed for whatever blessing was needed. When I then inquired of my friend
about his buddy Leo, I discovered that the day and hour of my
urging was the time of Leo's wedding. What small part in the
drama of Leo's life my prayer played I never found out and do
not need to know.

I experienced a seemingly more serious level of prayer when
my sister-in-law was rushed to the hospital for surgery on a brain
abscess. Nancy had never been a good surgical risk due to a con-
genital heart defect, and once again she was on the verge of
death. I pulled out the whole panoply of priestly arts for my
presurgery visit—vestments, Holy Communion, the formal
prayers of the church. When I arrived, I put my hands on her
head for a time of silent healing prayer. As I did, I felt surrounded by a circle of invisible "presences"—I can think of no
other term—and sensed that I should let these presences come
through me into Nancy. My inner theological screening committee awoke in a great quandary: *A circle of spirits? Who ever
heard of such a thing? Is this an approved form of Christian healing?
Surely this must be a figment of my imagination!*

Well, I reasoned, poised in midprayer, *Scripture says to "test the
spirits," and that's plural, so why couldn't this be?* (see 1 John 4:1).

The impression and subtle sense of presences continued, full of a sense of compassionate healing. That seemed to me to be in the Spirit of Christ, so I yielded myself to the impression of their passing through me into Nancy. No sooner had I surrendered to this process than its purpose seemed clear: *so she won't be alone on the operating table.*

Whether these presences were objectively real, a symbol of God's energies, or a fantasy I was having while praying, I simply don't know for sure. I know that Nancy survived the surgery, much to the astonishment of the medical staff. And I know that when I asked her afterward what spiritual resources she called upon as a repeated survivor of medical catastrophe, she said without hesitation, "Angels. It's as if there's a whole group of angels that sees me through, though until you asked, I hadn't really put it into words."

Suddenly I saw the obvious: how we need to companion one another inwardly, on the deep level of loving connection that intercessory prayer can provide, in all sorts of life situations. In the same way we can hold hands, hug, or give chicken soup or money, we need to support one another on the level of our inter-connected souls. No one should go into surgery or battle or even to a tough job interview alone on this level.

The day after the catastrophic terrorist attack on the World Trade Center, my wife stayed up late watching television news, in spite of my urging her to come to bed. The next morning she told me she had been looking for what to connect to on a prayer level in the tragedy. She couldn't pray for the "situation"; it was too over-whelming. After midnight, she saw the New York City fire chief tearfully reporting that over three hundred firefighters had been lost in the building collapse. "I knew then," she reported, "that it was my job to be with him." She meant not just in herself but in the light of God. In this light we behold ourselves and one another in that love that is both refiner's fire and healing balm.

Just as God carries us in the heart of the divine love (Ps. 28:9), so we carry one another in our hearts and minds—either as impressions to be ignored, disparaged, or worried over or as images to be befriended in love and offered to Love.

For ways to carry one another in prayer, see Exercises 4, 5, and 7 in the appendix.

CHAPTER 16

Learning to Pray with the World Again

Invoking the Creatures

The pressure of God's unfolding ecological judgment calls us to rediscover the earth as God has really made it rather than continue in the world of our own alienated consciousness. We are being called to carry earth in our hearts in humble recognition that we have, from the birth of our species onward, been carried in the interconnected web of Earth's life.

Earth's fabric, woven more of presences and powers than of impersonal forces, has at its heart a community of creatures of many species. These living presences continually call out for one another's presence, practicing invocations not only of God, the Great Spirit in all, but of one another as well.

Such invocation, or "calling in" of an element with which we are out of touch, involves seeing God's presence in other life forms and in the world around us. It can break through the isolation of our human chauvinism and recall us to our primal tasks as human beings. The old stories say we were created on the same day as the other animals and given the power to "name" them, thus entering deeply into relationship with them. We were called to be stewards of this world's life, not its plunderers.

According to both the Scriptures and the saints, this work of interspecies, ecological, and cosmic community is the world as God knows it. In it even worship is not limited to human hearts and minds but flows in cosmic song through all creatures. Saint Francis of Assisi moved naturally to the tones of this song. According to an eyewitness account, he was walking through the marshes of Venice when he came upon a flock of birds singing. He interpreted this act as the birds singing praise to God, so he invited the friar who was with him to "go in among them and chant the Lord's praises." They did, and the birds, remarkably, did not move; but their song was so loud that Francis and his companion could not hear each other. Francis kindly asked the birds to stop until he was finished. They quieted immediately and remained still until "the holy man of God gave them permission to sing again . . . , they immediately resumed singing in their usual way," according to Bonaventure, an early biographer.[1]

Bonaventure pictures Francis "calling creatures, no matter how small, by the name of brother or sister, because he knew they had the same source as himself."[2] Francis is only one of many holy men and women who have taken the creatures seriously.

Not considering myself much of an animal lover, I had never taken a nonhuman presence seriously until our cat snubbed me. Left in the house for a month's summer vacation, her every physical need had been met by our neighbor. Our cat did not greet our return, however, and actively avoided my presence. Then she confronted me at the kitchen table. Jumping up onto the magazine I was reading, she sat down in front of me, straight, still, glaring, without the trace of a purr. Very slowly she then got up, turned her back on me, and sat down decisively just out of reach, her back a wall between us. When I touched her, she stalked away. It took days of coaxing for her normally friendly attitude to return. She withheld her presence because we had withheld ours by deserting her.

If I had ever thought that animals were "dumb," I ceased to believe it at that moment. The last twenty years of research into mammalian brains and primate behavior have confirmed my conviction that our cat knew exactly what she was doing. Beginning with Jane Goodall's discoveries about chimpanzee communities, an increasing number of animal researchers speak openly about animal awareness, responsiveness, and even consciousness.

Later this same cat's behavior made me first consider the relation of the other creatures to the Spirit. Sitting deep in Centering Prayer, I became aware of something in front of me. Facing me as I sat on the floor, she purred, eyes downcast, sharing the silence, still as eternity, neither trying to be cuddled nor leaving until I was finished. Was this what the ancient canticle meant with the words, "O ye beasts and cattle, bless ye the Lord" (*Benedicite Omnia Opera*, 1979 BCP, 48)? The shell of my human-centered awareness had been cracked open to larger dimensions of the Spirit's work with creatures.

CREATURES, THE CREATOR, AND THE COSMIC COMMUNITY

With such ponderings, we begin to enter the world our distant ancestors knew intimately. This is a world where rock and stream, tree and field are understood to be alive, and all animals rejoice in the living God. When humans pray, earth and all its creatures are affected and God's presence on earth intensified.

This invocation of the creatures' presence is such a neglected art among Christians that it seems pagan to some when they hear of it. But the practice is as biblical as baptism and used to be a part of public worship. Not only do Psalms 104 and 147 celebrate the cosmic song, but the great hymn *Benedicite, Omnia Opera Domini*, "O All Ye Works of the Lord, Bless Ye the Lord" (from the Septuagint's additions to Daniel 3:23) appeared in the Eucharist in many early Western liturgies and has always had a prominent place in liturgical morning prayers.[3] These psalms and this hymn are surely vestiges of even earlier practices taken more seriously still in the ancient Hebrew world from which Christianity arose. We can also see how prominent this sense of cosmic community is in other forms of early Christianity, such as the Celtic church.

I bind unto myself today
The virtues of the starlit heaven,
The glorious sun's life-giving ray,
The whiteness of the moon at even,
The flashing of the lightning free,
The whirling wind's tempestuous shocks . . . [4]

Many environmentalists justly criticize Christian spirituality for its current separation from nature. Christians can recover their own past and reconnect their prayers to the cosmos without adopting pagan practices in the process. Reclaiming the sense of cosmic community will also lead to a deeper sympathy for the level of common truth Christians share with the spiritualities of the native peoples who are more faithful to this level of biblical insight than we are.

SAINTS AND THE CREATURES

The deepest part of our souls has not forgotten this world of interspecies community. Francis is the person whose soul was most awake to this cosmic connection in Christian tradition. His "brothers" and "sisters," the other creatures, were mysteriously drawn to him. Bonaventure speculates that the beasts "in some secret way" perceived the kind of feeling Francis had for them and were "attracted by his love," as in the case of a fish Francis addressed as brother. The fish hung about Francis's boat until dismissed by the holy man. Bonaventure also tells of a wild hare that came when Francis called and refused to leave him. Placed on the ground, the hare always came back until Francis had the brothers take it far away into the wilderness.

Prayer with a creature was natural to Francis. Once on the Lake of Rieti, one of the locals handed him a waterfowl recently trapped. The saint, of course, opened his hands to let the bird go, but it would not leave him. Holding the bird, Francis spent over an hour in contemplative prayer. The bird remained calm and still through this long meditation, then received Francis's blessing, and, upon being dismissed, "the bird expressed its joy in the movements of its body, and flew away."

If we cannot take these stories seriously, the problem may be ours. Bonaventure writes within the living memory of Francis's life. These are not artfully crafted symbolic stories but accounts of the effect a human soul profoundly rooted in God can have on other life-forms as well as on humans.[5]

The ancient lore has it that our first parents could communicate with the other animal species that share this garden planet with us. Not only could Eve and Adam understand animal speech, they also could speak directly to the souls of their fellow creatures to "call" them into relationship and to "name" or evoke some aspect of their being. The "other realm" Francis entered may indeed have been a deep level of interconnectedness that exists in the real world God is making among us and which our distant ancestors knew before their fall into our more alienated mode of being.

I have witnessed events in meditative prayer groups that parallel Francis's interconnectedness. Sitting outside at the local convent, group members have gone together into that wonderful still surge of silence that wells up so strongly when the group is willing to move into it. After a while, the birds sometimes swoop lower and hop nearer. The chipmunks and squirrels edge closer and sit for a while, poised and still, as if they can't quite believe these humans are being there, in their world, in this way.

A close friend of mine reported a notable phenomenon he observed at an ashram in rural India known for its deep communal meditation. It was not uncommon to find wild animals of all kinds sitting quietly on the grounds. "I had to wade through a flock of wild birds that refused to be alarmed by my presence, even though a similar flock miles from the ashram had taken off at my approach. And I myself could sense the palpable atmosphere of peace that dwelt in the place."

Learning how to be present in a calm, nonagitated manner is required for this reconciliation with the creatures to begin taking place. Better yet is a consciousness full of compassionate blessing that regards what is encountered receptively, not aggressively. The kind of presence Francis brought to animals develops in yet deeper levels of human prayer—not only the exterior silence but the interior silence that is one aim of contemplative prayer. In this kind of prayer, we may enter the depths of God's world again—a world in which the animals live. Animals seem to find peace in the presence of humans rooted in God. Until we carefully cultivate that foundation in God, "fear and dread" of us are upon every beast for good reason (Gen. 9:2). Possibly Isaiah's dream of the peaceable kingdom, where wolf and lamb live together (Isa. 11:6), arises from ancient experiences of this kind of animal behavior around holy places. Does Isaiah envision "zones of peace" rather than the unlikely prospect of a permanent truce between predator and prey?

Some animals seem to like human beings engaged in silent or chanted prayer. Our solitary prayer can be enriched by invocation of the creatures, just as it is by praying with other humans. The danger is that we moderns will merely personify nature, imagining it in our image. The presences we encounter in nature are all the more significant because they are not human. A man who encountered a moose eye-to-eye in a moment of mutual regard witnessed, "It was like looking into another world, both familiar and very different at the same time."

Animals confront us with ways of being present that differ from our own, not just a less developed version of our experience. They are "not underlings; they are other nations," as naturalist Henry Beston put it two generations ago. "In a world older and more complete than ours they move finished and complete, gifted with extensions of the senses we have lost or never attained, living by voices we shall never hear."[6]

LET THE TREES SING FOR JOY

This encounter with spiritual presence in nature goes even deeper down than our relationship with close animal cousins like mammals or birds. In the world experienced by the vision-aries who wrote Scripture, the whole realm of nature is spiritu-ally alive. They call the mountains and hills to join the praise and the trees of the forest to "sing for joy" when God comes to set right the earth (Ps. 96:12). The earth and the ocean themselves have "faces" (see Gen. 1:2, 29). The whole earth, in fact, is absolutely drenched with God's glory (Isa. 6:3).

Biblical people, like many aboriginal peoples the world over, had not yet dulled their senses to the spiritual dimensions of nature. The biblical language should not be dismissed as mere metaphor or poetic exaggeration by a modern world that has lost touch with the earth as God sees it. We can't really have any sense of what a huge boulder or great tree is unless we allow our-selves to be present, receptive, and prayerful in its presence.

Many years ago, at the depths of the depressive illness I suf-fered in my thirties, I found myself drawn again and again to touch plants, especially at sundown, when the depression always got worse. It made no rational sense to me, but I was too needy to let that stop me. I would hold the leaves of the ficus tree in our plant room as I cried, and it seemed as if a calmness flowed from the plant to soothe me, physically and emotionally, deep inside. I then found that sitting under the huge oak tree in the backyard with my back pressed against the trunk had an even more intense effect. Those plants helped me survive, I know not how. I don't imagine little tree sprites populate every tree, but I now understand why ancient people thought so, and I know that a tree can be an agent of the same God who uses other elements like wind and fire as messengers of grace (see Heb. 1:7). Our modern separation of animate and inanimate creatures and things was unknown to them. All aspects of the creation were "creatures" and part of the unending song of praise: "O ye fire and heat, bless ye the Lord" (*Benedicite Omnia Opera* 1:44, 1979 BCP, 48).

All humanity is being called to reawaken to the reality of nature's aliveness as the temple of the Spirit of God, to pray and act for earth's healing. God wove us from earth's elements "to serve and take care" of the planet (Gen. 2:15, RCM). Its needs are ours, its griefs we cannot ignore, and its prayer for healing we cannot refuse to join.

REENTERING EARTH'S PRAYER

According to Scripture, creation itself is praying as part of the sweep of God's own Spirit through the universe, "groaning" for redemption (Rom. 8:22). What would it be like to rejoin that prayer, to invoke the creatures as community when we pray? Invocation can be used outdoors as a way to be centered and open, still and receptive. We can drink in the distinctive quality of a special valley or mountain, waterfall or lake. As we spend time attending to the unique characteristics of the presence of this special place, we then go deeper into the God who fills both this place and the whole earth. We welcome whatever creatures choose to come and join us.

Invocation can be used as an interior act of the heart to place our prayer in the cosmos. We can call into our heart's imagining the various members of the cosmic community. Beginning with the vastness of the starry sky above us and the firm warmth of the bedrock below us, we can let our minds gaze over the variety of creatures we have encountered in person or in pictures, allowing the heart to linger on one special creature, letting the sense of mutual presence grow. Together in God's pervasive presence we can be still and know the One who is the Source of us all.

Such invocation can serve as the prelude to intercession. We begin to take God's own care and plan for the earth seriously. We let the Spirit join us in the common breath of the earth's full community, which "groans" under the burden of human sinfulness.

On the day I heard of the disastrous nuclear accident at Chernobyl with its vast cloud of radioactive contamination spreading across Europe, a deep moan arose from deep down within.

I found myself crying in sorrow for this assault on the land, the waters, and the creatures. I soon found myself lying on the earth in the backyard, turning my moaning and crying into a prayer of sorrow, repentance, and healing. While perhaps a bit dramatic, it was what my body wanted to do. Afterward I realized that prostrating oneself on the ground to worship the God of creation was exactly what biblical people did, among other ritual acts. Maybe our prayers need to get back in touch with the earth in more ways than one.

If we allow ourselves to respond to earth's groaning, we can be joined to the great act of birthing God is working in the earth, seeking to bring forth the true children of God, that is, human beings truly fit to be earth's guardians, aligned with God's own creative love (Rom. 8:22). Connected with the whole web of life, we begin to share God's sorrow, which is so in touch with the creatures that Jesus says God knows when a sparrow falls (Matt. 10:29). Our intercessions become part of the deep inner work that alone can birth the true image of God within us, the true stewards and priests of this planet's life.

The beasts and trees of the field wait for such children of God. These creatures pray in their own ways for that day when the earth and all the waters roar with praise, and the field and "everything in it" exults with joy before the God who "is coming to judge the earth" (Ps. 96:10-13), restoring the right relationship between humanity and the rest of creation (see Ps. 98:6-9).

In our day, the creatures wait for us to rejoin such prayer with increasing urgency.

For a meditative prayer to join God's own caring for the world, see Exercise 9 in the appendix.

CHAPTER 17

The Art of Unceasing Prayer

Growing Up into God's Life

Urgency for the well-being of the earth is born in the heart of God. The divine desire moves through the world, seeking to make all creatures radiant with goodness and alive with righteousness. True prayer includes every desire of our own that helps align us with this loving movement of the Spirit. Once we realize this, we're very close to prayer "without ceasing" (1 Thess. 5:17).

THE CONSTANT FLOW OF ORDINARY PRAYER

We are actually praying all the time without realizing it. There's a constant stream of hungers and needs, gripes and groans, desires and dreams that well up from the mysterious depths of soul and body, reaching out to connect with the life within us and around us. This semiconscious asking may not be addressed to God, but it is prayer nonetheless, deeper than and prior to any belief system. The ancient languages of the Bible witness to this truth, for the word translated "pray" actually signifies a wide range of ways to reach out: to petition, entreat, want, interrogate, call for, beseech, wish, whisper, pour out energy, smooth down, or give praise.[1]

Much of daily life involves this kind of praying. Human beings reach out to one another and to life itself with requests, complaints, confessions, blessings, praises, invocations, and communions. Our bodies "pray" for food or comfort and constantly

203

commune with the breath of life itself. We pray to ourselves, asking where we've left the keys or what we feel about something. Desires felt and desires met flow almost continuously. When we regard prayer from this angle, we can see that it's almost impossible for us to stop praying! The old hymn rightly claims that "prayer is the soul's sincere desire, unutter'd or expressed."[2]

Some forms of spirituality see desire as a problem to be solved, the fever to be stilled, a sign of innate self-centeredness. Desire-prayers are childish and immature, to be discarded as we aim for heights of contemplation free of desire's distractions.[3] Fortunately biblical spirituality invites desire into the light of God's presence. Jesus encourages us to be bold as we "ask . . . seek . . . knock" (Luke 11:9, KJV).

Desire needs to be educated, not eradicated. Prayer is designed to be our main way of sorting things out. How can our desires ever grow up if we keep hiding them from ourselves and from God? The woman praying for a mink coat may never get one but may discover, by bringing her desire into the light of God, that what she really wants, deep down, is to feel elegant and beautiful. There's probably a better way to fulfill that desire. The man who prays for a racy sports car may not get it, but if he really opens up his desiring to the Spirit's influence, he may discover the desire behind the desire: a renewed sense of youthful excitement. His prayer may lead to unexpected results—an invitation to coach a school soccer team or to get involved in working with teenagers.

Scripture promises that God will grant "the desires of your heart" (Ps. 37:4), but first we have to find it.

Many years ago I faced a vague but persistent unhappiness in parish ministry. Why was I so recurrently dissatisfied with a job that was, in so many ways, rewarding? Did this restlessness mean I should leave the ministry? What did I really want?

Following some sensible advice, I began reflecting on my major skills and interests. I took values-clarification tests and talked to mentors. Should I be a psychologist? a schoolteacher?

I even speculated about veterinary medicine as a total change of pace. Finally one day I took myself into deep prayer and laid out before God my bewilderment over all these confusing options. *What do you want me to do?* I virtually shouted. *Just let me know.*

Much to my astonishment, an answer came back loud and clear, resounding in my inmost mind, expressed with an incredible sense of courtesy and caring: *What do* you *want to do?* The way this inwardly heard Voice had said "you" conveyed such respect for the fabric of my being that I felt honored. Hearing this, I realized that expecting God to make such a decision was shirking my own responsibility. I needed to know my heart's desire and offer it to be woven into the divine purposes. In that moment I knew the answer to the Voice's question and blurted it out: *I'd really like to teach!*

In the next few weeks I was able to ponder and pray the different ways I might exercise a ministry of teaching spiritual development to adults. This led, in turn, to a moment of illumination and a clear sense of call about starting the interreligious learning center that has been the basis of my ministry for the last two decades.

Conventional teaching leads us to believe that "thy will be done" means our desire won't be honored. Sometimes that is the case, especially when our will is still captive to the more superficial cravings and fears of our nature. But it is God's pleasure to delight in our desires for the good. Major decisions in the early church were taken because it "seemed good to the Holy Spirit *and to us*" (Acts 15:28, italics added). "Thy will be done," quite precisely, includes learning to honor our deepest and most creative desires and finding joy in offering them to be part of God's work in the world.

KEEP ON ASKING

More than one spiritual teacher has advocated presenting every desire, no matter how unworthy, to God. The key is to stay connected with God as desire declares itself, consider what it really wants, and seeks the desire behind the desires. If we keep on asking, we keep our desiring and dreaming open to the light of the Spirit's commentary and correction. The Greek text of Jesus' famous "ask, seek, find" saying emphasizes this aspect; literally, it reads, "Keep on asking, keep on seeking, keep on knocking" (see Luke 11:9, RCM).[4]

Frustration often precedes clarification. I counseled a young mother whose hunger for further education had been awakened by a West Coast training institute's degree program. She saw that program as perfectly suited to her needs. She felt so clearly guided to pursue this institution's offering that she believed "surely everything will work out." It didn't. Moving to the West Coast was totally unfeasible for her family. "But the guidance seemed so clear!" she protested. Baffled and hurt, she gave up on neither her desire nor her prayer. Eventually she was led to a new, more feasible, local master's degree program. Desire, disappointment, and refining prayer had led to discovery and the eventual fulfillment of desire.

OUR DESIRES AND GOD'S CREATING

The deepest mystery of human desiring is that it springs from the Divine itself. We do not create our desires for beauty, compassion, justice, love, peace, and excellence. They create us.

In many ways, we've gotten the direction of prayer backward: What we call prayer actually begins with God, not with us (see Rom. 8:26). It wells up out of God's own desires for the ongoing life of the world. God prays to us and through us, calling us to join the divine desires for a world radiant with glory and for human lives strong enough to thrive in such an atmosphere. Our participation in that ongoing prayer begins in the depths of our unconscious when a divine desire stirs our own desiring. As Saint Paul puts it, the Spirit wants to work with and through our deepest and truest desires, moving through us with "sighs too deep for words," opening our lives to God (see Rom. 8:26-28).

A new young mother, alone for the first time with her baby, finds herself at her wit's end. Husband away on a business trip, mother gone home, she feels increasingly helpless as the crying infant is not comforted by her efforts. A cry comes up from the belly, "O God, please help me!" Then, as Jean described it to our spiritual sharing group, "I was overwhelmed with a ferocious love for this beautiful, squalling baby. I had never felt anything like it in my life. As I stood there, weeping, loving my baby, I realized I was surrounded by God, radiating the same love for me. I knew that my love for my child was but a piece of God's love." The baby continued to squall, but the mother, no longer alone, was renewed in her ability to love.

Jean's prayer had begun with God's own "groaning" deep within her soul, opening her to a love that would give her more than she consciously prayed for. We're mostly unconscious of these deeper processes. Usually our prayers seem to begin with a stubbed toe, a challenge we're facing, or some other need in our own life or in the life of someone we love. Or prayers may seem to well up out of gratitude for blessing. But our prayers are ultimately rooted in the God whose image we bear.

PRAYER IS CONNECTION WITH AN ACTIVE GOD

As our desiring and God's desiring weave together, our lives begin to find their place in the light of God's love and purposes for the world. Prayer connects heart, mind, and body to a generous Spirit that stands ready to move through any available opening, bestowing whatever goodness may be possible in any given situation.

This truth about prayer came home to me quite dramatically some years ago when I drove over hilly terrain on an icy day to teach a class. I set out with a prayer to be alert and careful; the trip over the hills was slippery but uneventful. On the way home, I commended the journey to God but in a more relaxed way, thinking the rising temperature had melted all the ice. Halfway down a steep hill in the dark, a subtle but urgent warning rose up within me, more in feelings than words: *Watch out!* I slowed down, wondering if I was approaching a hidden patch of ice. Once again the warning, *Stop!* As I slammed on the brakes, my rational mind expecting to go into an icy skid, an almost invisible black car pulled out right in front of me from a side road. Had I not been braking at that moment, the two cars would have collided.

If I had not been prayerfully open already, I might not have heeded the rather subtle inner warning. I realized on that dark hill that praying for God's protection means staying in touch with the God who might be able to offer guidance in a dangerous situation. We do not have to beg graces from a God who already knows our needs before we ask (see Matt. 6:8). We can grow in trusting a God who is more ready to give than we to receive. Openness is the secret that allows the Spirit room to act.

The importance of openness in prayer was raised quite poignantly right after the terrorist attacks on the World Trade Center at a community forum about dealing with trauma. A man said that he had to rethink all his ideas about God and prayer because, "after all, what good did prayer do for all those people who died in the collapse of the twin towers?" The man's level of pain made any stock answer impossible. I took a deep prayer-breath, opened myself to Wisdom, and found myself saying, "It's like water filling a sponge." I was thinking of one of those tiny little flat sponges that expand remarkably when filled with water.

"Prayer immerses you in Spirit like the sponge is immersed in water. Things inside you start opening up and becoming more flexible, soft and pliant and usable, like the fabric and holes of the sponge. When we don't avail ourselves of prayer, something deep in both soul and body dries up like the dry sponge—less flexible, less spacious inside. That means our responses to life may be less resourceful, less resilient, less buoyed by grace, less ready for inspiration. With prayer, even the situations we face seem to become more flexible, more malleable, and more open to grace. Like seasoning added to food, prayer brings out the essential goodness hidden in any situation more strongly. We cannot control the form in which God's goodness will appear."

We'll never know how many people got out of the World Trade towers because they opened their hearts prayerfully. Prayer helped people keep their heads clear, inspired them to help others, and opened some to see ways around obstacles they might have missed otherwise. Furthermore, we will never know how being connected to Spirit might have made a difference in the final moments for some people caught without any possibility of escape in the buildings' collapse.

I recalled the experience of my habitually prayerful friend Rabbi Shefa Gold after a catastrophic car accident. She regained consciousness in great pain but felt simultaneously surrounded by a "cushion" of the Spirit's presence supporting and sustaining her. She knew in whose hands she lay, and this knowledge was an inexpressible comfort. Prayer had made even this terrible situation more spacious.

Prayer isn't getting God to do something; it's allowing God to move through our active receptivity to work with and through us in our deepest desires and needs to bring forth the highest possible good in any situation. Spiritual growth entails the gradual process of realizing that every moment and aspect of our lives happens in the Divine's presence and is called to be part of the divine movement. What may begin with a blessing for a stubbed toe or a thanksgiving for a beautiful sight is meant, finally, to include everything, so that God's presence becomes as natural to us as light and air. As we grow spiritually, we learn to see our lives happening in the context of God's all-surrounding Life.

THE "INSEPARABLE THIRD"

As I was writing this book, I had a dream about this all-pervasive Presence:

> In a beautiful meadow, surrounded by lush woods, I'm teaching a man and woman how to awaken their souls

and bodies to the world around them. First I show them
how to know the feeling of each other's presence. Next
they learn how to extend their senses to feel the
landscape and creatures around them: the aliveness
of the grass, the calm of the trees, the movement of the
animals. Then I say to them, "Open yourselves more.
Feel the Inseparable Third." This "Third" is a subtle
Aliveness in which everything else is alive, inseparable
from everything else but vastly larger. It is like a silent
music resonating through everything. As intimate as the
constant, unnoticed touch of the air, it is a surrounding,
silent Knowing. "There," I say. "Do you feel it? It's always
there. Let it be there as a constant background."

I don't usually have clear dreams like this, certainly not ones
that lay out a course of instruction in mystical meditation. But
there it was, a commentary in the night as I wrestled with the
final chapters of this book, expressing what I have been trying
to communicate, the art of cultivating a constantly recurring
awareness of God's all-surrounding, persistent grace.

The dream immediately reminded me of another dream that
came as a puzzling surprise in my mid-twenties:

I am in some paradisiacal, heavenly place, surrounded by
a large circle of people. Some are strangers, but quite a
few are people I know and love. A Light at once both
strong and gentle shines on us all, flowing over us from
everywhere. I wonder where God is and realize that I'm
not going to see God because God can't be seen. Rather,
I'm seeing all these people in this radiant Light that
flows from the everywhere God, and which is, somehow,
God's own seeing. We are meant to see each other, and
everything, in the Light of God.

In the end, most lives are not about anything very heroic, in
the sense of making a big splash in history. A few great souls

make a big impact, of course, but that impact's effect entirely depends on its penetration into our more ordinary, nonspectacular lives.

Whenever our praying links with God's desiring, our spirits become full of God's own life flowing through us. The smallest deed, done as blessing, moves the world one step closer to its own deepest hopes and dreams. And our own spirits taste the joy for which they are made.

We wake and work and sleep. We love and fight and reconcile. We invest energy in the work of the world and shape it slightly toward good or ill. We're born, we grow, we die. What matters in the end is how we live these ordinary, daily events. They are the weaving of the world.

For suggestions on pondering the relationship of human desiring and God's desires, see Exercise 10 in the appendix.

A Prayer
for Walking in Grace

May I walk this day
in the realm of grace,
walking with You
my feet firmly on your earth-path,
my heart loving all as kindred,
my words and deeds alive with justice.

May I walk as blessing,
meeting blessing at every turn
in every challenge, blessing,
in all opposition, blessing,
in harm's way, blessing.

May I walk each step in this moment of grace,
alert to hear You
and awake enough to say
a simple Yes.

APPENDIX

MEDITATIVE PRAYER EXERCISES

Prayer is a natural human instinct and ability. No training is required to reach God, only a trusting openness. Like all human abilities, however, this natural ability can be trained into greater strength and suppleness. Just as we can learn the arts of courtesy, attentiveness, and communication with other humans, we can learn the art of greater openness to grace. These meditative prayer exercises spell out, step-by-step, acts of prayer and meditation described in the book. Each exercise is best practiced from ten to twenty minutes. But even five minutes spent in practice is a step toward deeper relationship with God.

EXERCISE 1

A Prayer of Simple Focus: Practicing Mindfulness

For centuries, people of all faiths have used the universal practice of breath awareness to evoke a shift in mind and body toward relaxed focus and alert openness.

1. Arrange the body in your chosen posture of prayer. Sitting is ordinarily the best posture for meditative prayer. Some find kneeling while sitting back on the heels or a low meditation bench (available from some religious orders) helpful. The posture should be comfortable, with spine erect—in order to quiet the body and free the awareness for openness to God. Many people find it helpful to rest the hands, palms face up and open, in a gesture of openness. This ancient posture of prayer was common for Jews, Christians, and pagans alike.

2. Follow the breath, closing your eyes and actively sensing the inflow and outflow of the stream of air. Sense the vast ocean of air that surrounds you. Let heart and mind silently acknowledge this as the moment-by-moment gift of life from the Breath of Life. As it is written, God breathed into our nostrils God's own breath, and we became living beings (Gen. 2:7).

3. Let a short prayer phrase join each breath in your mind, such as one of the following:

> "I am—Thou art" or "I am—You are."
> "Here—am I" or "Here—I am."
> "Lord Jesus, Son of God—have mercy on me."

The phrase can be divided between the in-breath and the out-breath or said silently in the mind on the out-breath. (If continuing to focus on the breath seems uncomfortable, simply focus on the phrase.)

4. As distractions arise (and they will!), "passively disregard them," as Harvard doctor Herbert Benson advises. As a noise intrudes, an emotion or image arises inside the mind and you notice that your attention turns toward the noise. On the next in-breath, simply refocus on the phrase. Gradually more of your conscious awareness becomes, quite simply, present and open to the Presence.

5. As this practice of mindfulness deepens, you may choose to let go of the prayer phrase and simply let the breath focus your awareness: here, now, in this moment. Bring your full attention to whatever you are perceiving, doing, or feeling. Let it be, without judgment, and savor it.

EXERCISE 2
Bathing in the Light of God

1. After "centering down" and opening yourself to the Spirit's guidance, imagine yourself in a place that is holy for you. It may be a church, a natural setting, or any location where you can be open to an encounter with Christ—or with the Spirit of God. (Throughout this meditation you may prefer to use the aspect of Spirit or simply God rather than the more specific image of Christ.)

2. Imagine a sunburstlike globe of Light in front of you, radiant and alive. Within that globe let the Christ begin to appear in a human form but still Light. You can let your image of Christ become very realistic, like reverent portraits you've seen, or you can let the shining humanity remain less distinct.

3. Reverently approach this Light with a prayer. Enter the Light-Body of Christ, turning so that you are surrounded by the Light or clothed in Christ's nature. Let it suffuse you. Let the Light do as it wishes with your body, your feelings, your thoughts. You may find yourself feeling as if you are, for a while, "becoming Christ." You may, conversely, remain distinct and react to the Light.

4. Imagine that your own heart is shining with this Light. Deep within the center of your chest, let a heart-space form, sparked into fresh aliveness by its saturation in God's own light.

5. When it feels appropriate, remember your own shape and appearance clearly. Begin remembering the actual physical location where you are.

6. Thank the Living Light of God for whatever graces you have received and let the light fade around you, remembering that it "shines in the darkness, and the darkness did not overcome it" (John 1:5).

EXERCISE 3
Breathing the Breath of God

We live in a culture full of physically and spiritually deadening practices—pushing too hard, ignoring our God-woven flesh, suppressing feelings. Even early Christians saw with penetrating insight that "the wages of sin"—being out of alignment with the Life-Giver—deadens. The following cleansing exercise aims to allow what mystic Charles Williams calls "the holy and glorious Flesh" to get out from under the burden of our ego-driven lives and into the ordered freedom of the Spirit's enlivening grace.

1. Begin by using a nonverbal breath prayer—focusing on the inflow and outflow of your breathing. As thoughts and concerns come to your mind, passively disregard them. Thoughts come and go; you keep returning to focus on the Breath of Life. Let each breath become, ever so slowly, a deeper drink of the boundless vitality of the Breath of Life itself.

2. Imagine you can feel the vitality of the Breath of Life moving through your lungs like a gentle breeze. . . . You breathe in the vitality deeply. . . . You feel this vitality fill you up completely. . . . You feel the refreshing, cleansing outflow of the breath, carrying with it all that needs to leave your body. With each exhale you let go of whatever needs to be released right now.

3. As thoughts and images, memories and concerns arise in your mind, begin to note them, then let them go at the next exhale. If a memory with an emotional charge arises, let that simply be, passively disregarding the pull to go into the emotional swirl, by focusing on the next exhale. If a memory,

pleasant or unpleasant, keeps presenting itself, continue letting it go with each exhale. Note: It is vitally important not to
fight the strong emotion that may arise from this exercise.
Simply note it, let it be, and then refocus on the exhale.

4. If a memory is especially difficult and persistent, there are
two options:

    a) Let the cleansing flow of the divine Breath move
       through the memory of the emotion. You may or may
       not note changes in the emotion and its physical
       effects.

    b) Refocus on the breath and add a verbal prayer: "Kyrie
       eleison" or "Lord, let your love shine" or "Breathing
       God within" or a phrase of your own choice.

5. At the end of the prayer time, offer the whole experience up
to the continued working of grace in your life.

EXERCISE 4
Using the Names of God

God may indeed be present everywhere, but we are not always present to God. The basic meditative skill of centering the awareness allows our consciousness to turn toward the Spirit and our deeper selves to become more present to the grace already available.

A. THROUGH RECITATION

Recitation of one of the divine names is an ancient and universal spiritual practice, now revived as "Centering Prayer." This outline uses the full Hebrew form of Jesus' name—*YAHOSHUA* (*YAH*, "God, is salvation"). Any of the multitude of names in scripture, tradition, and human experience of grace may be used in its place, such as, O Shepherd, O Mother, O Wisdom, *El Shaddai.*

1. Center and focus your awareness by letting your attention dwell on your breathing, receiving, and giving back the Breath of Life.

2. Let a sacred name you have chosen join each breath, as you repeat it inwardly in your mind: *Living God, Merciful Christ, Strong Mother,* or any of the many names from sacred text, tradition, and spontaneous inspiration. The name of Jesus has been used since apostolic times in this way. In Hebrew, the powerful sounds of *Yahoshua* suggest both the open, spacious nature of divine grace (the *ah* in *Yah*), and the Spirit's windlike blowing of healing energy (the *hoshhhh* in *hosua*). As distractions arise, gently note them, let them go, and return to the sacred name. Let yourself continue for 10 to 15 minutes. Conclude with silent gratitude and openness to the Presence.

B. Through invocation

Invocation of the name means calling upon some aspect of God to be present in your consciousness so you can make an intentional alliance with it.

1. Repeat steps one and two from above.

2. Now add to this name to express a need or desire more fully. *"Kyrie Iesus eleison!"* is a traditional Christian prayer phrase that means, "Lord Jesus, have mercy!" Be open and ready to learn appropriate names for differing needs, for example, "Bright Joy, lift me from darkness."

C. As blessing

1. Repeat steps one and two from "Recitation" above.

2. Now enfold a person or concern into a phrase using a sacred name:

    > "May the Merciful Compassion relieve Susan's burden of guilt."
    > "Holy Calm and Peace be upon Jim today."
    > "El Shaddai's wings cover you in your danger, Mary!"
    > "Yahoshua's healing pervades your body and soul, Bill."

3. Keep repeating the blessing with each breath. You might also choose to envision the person being blessed.

EXERCISE 5

Meditation for Distress, Disease, or Pain

God's resurrection promise in Christ is shalom—active, bountiful goodness. "Shalom I give you, not as the ordinary world gives it" (John 14:27, paraphrase). Such bountiful goodness can flow around, through, and under any situation. Living with disease, difficulty, or distress can sometimes be as important as curing it. Often just learning to live with the difficulty constitutes the first stage in a cure! However experienced—as light, as peace, as minor relaxation in the midst of pain, as comfort, as assurance, or as growing health—shalom comes from the Spirit itself, the Source of all goodness. A meditation such as the following one can open flesh, soul, and spirit to the Spirit's grace, which is already more available than we realize.

1. Let the body be as comfortable as possible, whether you are standing, sitting, or lying down. Close your eyes.

2. Spend a few minutes "following the breath," that is, consciously turning your attention to the moment-by-moment inflow and outflow of air through nostrils or mouth. The simple act of focusing on only one thing at a time immediately invites a deeper "relaxation response" from your body, whether you feel it consciously or not. If conscious awareness of the breath makes you nervous, then use a short prayer phrase, like "Lord, have mercy" or "God is good," repeated affirmatively over and over.

3. Imagine that a gentle, strong light surrounds you, as if the air around you were a cloud of light. Imagine the light as any color you wish, so long as it carries positive and supportive associations. Remember that "God is Light" and that this imagined light can be a symbol and sacrament of that reality.

4. Slowly let the light begin to pervade your entire being. Gently, soothingly, your whole physical self and field of consciousness are suffused with this healing light. You may even start to breathe it in. If you are praying about a situation, imagine the light suffusing that situation and all the people in it.

5. Let the light find the hurting and needy places by allowing your imagination to flow freely. What happens may surprise you. Don't expect every ache and pain to go away. But let the Light have its way with you for a while. "Marinate" yourself in God's goodness. Then, with a long slow breath, give thanks for whatever good you have noted.

EXERCISE 6

Discerning God's Presence in Daily Life

God is present in every situation of our lives, but we often are not aware of that constant presence. We can learn to be open to what Tilden Edwards calls the "graced edge" of any experience by using our whole brain to bring an experience back for review or spiritual examen. Sometimes the grace we encounter is pleasant and warm; sometimes it is challenging and severe. But always it is God-with-us.

1. As you take a few long, slow breaths, let your awareness begin to dwell on your breathing. Attuned to the sensation of receiving life by inhaling the breath of life and letting go into Life through the exhale, make an inner intention to turn your heart and mind to God. Take a few moments with this process.

2. Invite into the open space in your awareness a memory of a recent event that seemed graced in some way. Perhaps it was a time of manifest goodness or a time full of challenge.

3. Use all your senses to recall that event as vividly as possible. Relive it, seeing the surroundings, other people involved, how you were dressed. Recall the feeling, or tone, of the situation and reconnect with the emotions or thoughts you may have been having. What sensations and feelings did your body experience? Were any odors noticeable? Did you have any sense of God's presence?

4. Now use all your imaginative senses to see how God may be present in this scene, though you "knew it not." If the Divine were tangibly manifest in this scene, how would God be pres-

ent? What sounds, colors, shapes, figures or forms, light or energy would God use to make known the living Presence? What "names" or titles of God come to mind to describe this Presence? Let your soul be free to "see" without judgment or restriction. Receive your soul's impressions gracefully.

5. After you have finished the imaginal process, spend some time reflecting on your impressions. Compare what you have remembered imaginatively with images of the Divine in Scripture and Christian experience through the ages. If something seems unusual or strange, you may wish to do some research to see if this aspect of God is simply unfamiliar to you. Be welcoming but not uncritical about your impressions and "test the spirit" of them for their congruence with the Spirit of Christ.

EXERCISE 7

The Compassionate Connection:
Caring for Another in Prayer

1. Begin by going through steps 1–4 of Exercise 1. Or use a centering method of your own.

2. When you have "centered down" in your own impression of the breath and light of God, bring the person for whom you wish to pray into your mind. Imagine the person as vividly as you can, as if he or she were standing or sitting before you in that light of God that surrounds you.

3. Let that light shine on the individual, surround and pervade the person. See the person in a positive, healthy state without trying in any further way to "make him/her better."

4. You may find it helpful to add a prayer affirmation, perhaps connected to the inflow and outflow of your breathing:

    "May God bless you, _____."
    "Light around you, light within you, _____."
    "Christ within you, _____."

5. You also may wish to talk to the person, here in the Light, with words of encouragement and expressions of care. (Any words at this point are meant to be blessings, vehicles of your caring, affirmations of God. No lecturing, correcting, coercing.)

6. Conclude by letting go. Offer the prayer, your feelings, and the images to God.

Here are two variations on this exercise:

A. Work through difficult personal relationships by being with the difficult person "in the Light." Let yourself be open to seeing the person more clearly and visualizing God's blessing shining on her or him.

B. Be more specific in your visualization of a sick or troubled person's becoming better. You might "see" an individual's immune system absorbing and taking away infection, a wound or incision healing, cancer shrinking under proper treatment. If you follow this method, don't strain or push. Let the Light itself do these positive things.

EXERCISE 8

Following Jesus' Challenges in Daily Life

As chapter 4 suggests, the teachings of Jesus can be pondered one-by-one and embodied in one's life. Over the years I have distilled some steps that allow Jesus' words to "abide" in us (John 15:7).

1. Make a list of four or five of Jesus' most important challenges. Start with the ones most familiar to you.

2. List identifiable behaviors (action and attitude choices) that embody each teaching.

3. List identifiable instances of inability or unwillingness to embody each teaching.

4. Soberly note which of these specific teachings need more attention in your life and pick one. Don't bother with guilt. Guilt may lead to outward conformity but does not spur inner change. Just admit, "I'm not very good at that." Consider this the next "cutting edge" teaching for a growing soul.

5. Ponder two or three ways in which practicing this teaching might improve your life and relationships. If need be, seek out information or counsel about this teaching.

6. Brainstorm ways in which you could live out this teaching.

7. Choose one specific behavior at a time for intentional practice.

8. Seek out people who may know more about practicing this teaching than you do.

9. As you hear and read Scripture, be open for new challenges in Jesus' teaching you had not noticed before and add them to your list.

10. Aim for lifelong learning!

EXERCISE 9
Praying for the World

1. Relax with a few deep breaths, using the rhythm of your breathing to center your awareness here, now, in the present moment.

2. Intentionally open yourself to the flow of the Spirit of God through your heart, mind, and body. Many people use the image of breathing the Breath of Life or sitting surrounded by the Light of God.

3. Envision the entire planet before you, as we have all seen it through the eyes of the astronauts. You may choose to be realistic in your envisioning, using all your senses to imagine the earth's dappled blue oceans, rust-red-green continents, dazzling polar ice caps, and swirling cloud formations. Or you may prefer to see the whole planet more symbolically—as a political map, for instance, or by imagining differing populations of flora, fauna, and people.

4. Envision the whole planet being bathed in a visual symbol of God's compassionate love for all creatures—a great Light that streams from above or with a strong but gentle Wind that bathes, moves, cleanses, nourishes, and heals. Let this Light or Wind envelop you also and join your own caring compassion with the flow of the Spirit's intercession for the world.

5. Affirm the living "communion of saints" who care, pray, and work for the good of the world by imagining dots of light appearing like small stars all over the world. Let these lights connect into a web of light that girdles the globe, reminding you that your prayer joins a tide of prayer already happening.

6. You may wish to "zoom in" on particular situations or locations, moving imaginatively into a place where there is need or trouble. In each case, envision the difficulty sufficiently to be in touch with it but let your focus be on the Spirit, Light, or Wind that is moving through the situation.

   (Emphasize affirming God's presence and movement rather than ego-efforts to "fix" whatever is amiss. If, in the spontaneous movement of your images, you "see" people responding to the Light, affirm that with a silent "So be it!")

7. Conclude with the vision of the planet from space and a short verbal affirmation of your intention that "God's will be done on earth as it is in heaven." Offer the prayer with all its images and feelings to God as you understand God. Let it go into the divine Compassion.

EXERCISE 10

Our Desires and God's Desires

"Where your treasure is, there your heart will be also" (Matt. 6:21). As we pray and act, a conscious spirituality opens up dialogue between our desires and God's desires for us. It is not always a matter of my desires versus God's desires. Jesus declares that good comes out of the Law, not just love: "The good person out of the good treasure of the heart produces good, and the evil person out of evil treasure produces evil; for it is out of the abundance of the heart that the mouth speaks" (Luke 6:45).

Thomas Aquinas said that our prime motivation is to seek the good, even when we are mistaken about what it is. Thus, spiritual growth involves gradually sifting our deepest, truest desires from our powerful but superficial, distorted cravings. In touch with the good treasure of a heart made in the image of God, our lives can arrange themselves in cooperation with the Divine desires.

1. Make two lists in parallel columns:

    My recurrent deep desires   God's revealed desires for me

    _____   _____

    _____   _____

    _____   _____

    _____   _____

2. Compare and contrast the two lists and spend some time pondering how your recurrent desires shape your life and attitude, create "scripts," and help or hinder your relationship with the Spirit.

3. Conclude with a time of meditative prayer, summarizing your feelings through a free-flowing conversation with God or by repeating a prayer-phrase like "Thy love be done in me"; "Thy peace come in me"; or "Thy courage flow through me." Add phrases drawn from your list.

NOTES

Part One: Opening to Grace

1. This lovely verse is not found in all ancient manuscripts, and is now completely omitted from some translations. It is, however, a magnificent summary of Jesus' whole relationship with his disciples, and comes from the heart of his central teachings.

Chapter 1. The Second Breath: Frustration as a Doorway to Spiritual Practice

1. James Hillman, *The Soul's Code: In Search of Character and Calling* (New York: Random House, 1996), 88.

2. These meanings were taught by my Old Testament professor, the Reverend Robert C. Dentan at the General Theological Seminary in the 1960s. Also, E. A. Speiser, *Genesis*, The Anchor Bible (Garden City, N.Y.: Doubleday & Co., 1964), 24: "The basic meaning of [the Hebrew] *'rr* is 'to restrain (by magic), bind (by a spell).'" Conversely, blessing implies the rich sense of life abundant carried by the Greek *makarios*, "blessed," and *makarizo*, "to make blessed," especially by a "good word," *eulogia*.

3. "We know that the whole creation has been groaning in labor pains until now; . . . but we ourselves . . . groan inwardly" (Rom. 8:22-23). This way of looking at Saint Paul's famous "groaning in travail" passage links with the approach of archetypal psychologists James Hillman (*The Soul's Code: In Search of Character*

and Calling) and Thomas Moore (*Care of the Soul: A Guide for Cultivating Depth and Sacredness in Everyday Life*). They advocate "befriending" our darker impulses, seeking to understand their blind search for good, even as we restrain our behavior.

4. See James 3:10-13. "From the same mouth come blessing and cursing. . . . Does a spring pour forth from the same opening both fresh and brackish water?. . . Show . . . gentleness born of wisdom." All biblical Wisdom literature counsels careful watch of the words of power we use, both for their effect on our souls and on other people.

5. Pioneered by Norman Shealy, M.D., and popularized by Jon Kabat-Zinn in his book *Wherever You Go, There You Are: Mindfulness Meditation in Everyday Life* (New York: Hyperion, 1994).

6. Kathleen Norris, *The Cloister Walk* (New York: Riverhead Books, 1996), 213.

7. Friedrich von Hügel, *Selected Letters* (London: Dent, 1927), 269.

Chapter 2. Available Grace

1. See Arthur J. Deikman, "Mental Health, Aging, and the Role of Service," *The Harvard Mental Health Letter*, vol. 17, no. 8 (February 2001): 4–6.

2. See Herbert Benson, M.D., with Marg Stark, "Wired for God," in *Timeless Healing: The Power and Biology of Belief* (New York: Simon & Schuster, 1996), 195–217.

3. See Agnes Sanford, *The Healing Light* (St. Paul, Minn.: Macalester Park Publishing Co., 1965), 28.

4. Alexander Carmichael, *Carmina Gadelica: Charms of the Gaels, Hymns and Incantations*, ed. C. J. Moore (Hudson, N.Y.: Lindisfarne Press, 1994), 199, prayer 226.

5. For a fuller discussion of how to find the "graced edge" of daily life, see the whole of Tilden Edwards, *Living Simply through the Day: Spiritual Survival in a Complex Age* (New York: Paulist Press, 1977).

6. I am grateful to have been schooled in this Benedictine idea by Sister Donald Corcoran of the Camaldolese Benedictines.

7. See Thomas Keating, *Open Mind, Open Heart: The Contemplative Dimension of the Gospel* (New York: Continuum, 1996).

8. See Karen Armstrong, *A History of God: The 4000-Year Quest of Judaism, Christianity and Islam* (New York: Alfred A. Knopf, 1993), 196.

9. Ibid., 120–21.

10. Such experiences of Light are common enough in Christian spirituality to have a technical name, *photisms.*

Chapter 3. Meeting Grace on Its Own Terms

1. Vladimir Lossky, *The Mystical Theology of the Eastern Church* (London: James Clarke & Co., 1957), 76.

2. See Perle Epstein, *Kabbalah: The Way of the Jewish Mystic* (Boston, Mass.: Shambhala, 1988), 14–17. I have used the word *creativity* to clarify the meaning of the usual term, *foundation,* in the Tree of Life schema.

3. See *Julian of Norwich: Showings,* trans. Edmund Colledge and James Walsh (New York: Paulist Press, 1978), 133.

4. "Invocation" by Roberta Francis. Unpublished. Used by permission.

5. This idea was first introduced to me by the late Dr. Normal Pittenger, professor of Christian apologetics at the General Theological Seminary, whose teaching was based on that of Baron von Hügel, the early twentieth-century Catholic spiritual master.

6. Based on Exodus 20:21, there is a rich Christian experience of the divine Darkness, especially in the Eastern Church. See Kenneth Leech, "God of Cloud and Darkness" in *Experiencing God: Theology as Spirituality* (San Francisco: Harper & Row Publishers, 1985), 162–98.

7. Logion 5, Gospel of Thomas (RCM, author translation). Many New Testament scholars now consider Thomas, one of the

noncanonical Gospels, an important source of memories of Jesus' sayings. See Willis Barnstone, ed., *The Other Bible* (San Francisco: Harper & Row Publishers, 1984).

8. Isaiah 45:7 pictures God as the Source of both creation and destruction—indeed, the ultimate Source of all things. Hindu tradition is very clear in identifying the Divine as Creator and Destroyer. This is especially embodied in the image of Shiva, the third person of the Hindu Trinity, who dances in a circle of flame, creating and re-creating the world.

Chapter 4. Growing into the Image of God

1. See Perle Epstein, *Kabbalah,* especially pp. 14–17. The Kabbalistic lists were inspired by Old Testament lists like the one in 1 Chronicles 29:11: "Yours, O LORD, are the greatness, the power, the glory, the victory, and the majesty; for all that is in the heavens and on the earth is yours; yours is the kingdom, O LORD, and you are exalted as head above all."

2. For a fictional glimpse of first-century Jewish mysticism, see Bruce Chilton, *Rabbi Jesus: An Intimate Biography* (New York: Doubleday, 2000). While I disagree entirely with Chilton's reconstruction of Jesus' life-story, his portrait of first-century Jewish spirituality is well-founded.

3. "One Step at a Time," in *Sacred Selections for the Church* (Kendallville, Ind.: Sacred Selections Publishers, 1960), no. 210.

4. The Jesus of the Gospel of John says to us, "You are gods" (John 10:34), interpreting a reference to the angels in Psalm 82:6 to refer to human beings. Echoing this, Saint Athanasius of Alexandria taught that "the Divine became human that humanity might become God." Eastern Orthodox tradition talks boldly about *apotheosis,* the process of "divinizing" by which our small selves begin to live in harmony as the sacramental bearers of the divine love.

Chapter 5. The Altar of the Everyday

1. The original form of these Morning Blessings can be found in any *siddur,* or Jewish prayer book. See *Gates of Prayer: The New Union Prayerbook* (New York: Central Conference of American Rabbis, 1975), 286–87. This translation and wording is my own, inspired by similar reworkings of the prayers in contemporary Jewish renewal.

2. See Tilly-Jo Emerson and Robert Corin Morris, *Nourishing Spirituality in Congregations* (Interweave, 1999), available at www.interweave.org or P.O. Box 1516, Summit, NJ 07901, for examples of how to deepen the spiritual dimensions of work. Or contact Marshall, Towell and Emerson, Inc., 17 Woodland Rd., Maplewood, NJ 07040.

3. For information about Rabbi Gold's interreligious ministry, C-DEEP, see www.rabbishefagold.com.

4. Larry Dossey, M.D., *Healing Words: The Power of Prayer and the Practice of Medicine* (San Francisco: HarperSanFrancisco, 1993), especially appendix 1, 211 ff.

5. See Kenneth Ring and Evelyn Elsaesser Valarino, *Lessons from the Light: What We Can Learn from the Near-Death Experience* (Portsmouth, N.H.: Moment Point Press, 2000), especially chapter 1 and pp. 162–63.

Chapter 6. The Dangers of Religion

1. For a thorough treatment of the problem of the suppression of the shadow in religious practice, see John A. Sanford, *The Kingdom Within: The Inner Meaning of Jesus' Sayings,* rev. ed. (San Francisco: HarperSanFrancisco, 1987).

2. See Neil Douglas-Klotz, trans., *Prayers of the Cosmos: Meditations on the Aramaic Words of Jesus* (San Francisco: HarperSanFrancisco, 1990), 35, 71.

Chapter 7. Holy Fear and the Wildness of God

1. The Hebrew, in fact, makes a number of distinctions. To hold in reverence *(yare)* is not the same as to be afraid *(gur, dechal, yagor)* or to dread *(pachad)*. While all can be used to speak of the "fear of God," the most common is *yare*. In New Testament Greek, one word, *phobeo,* "to be afraid, to fear," must stand for all the forms of fear.

2. Classical Eastern Orthodox spirituality understands "watch and pray" (Matt. 26:41, KJV) as an invitation to vigilance or "watchfulness," both for the presence of God and the activity of spiritual danger. See the interesting discussion of this tradition in Robin Amis, *A Different Christianity: Early Christian Esotericism and Modern Thought* (Albany, N.Y.: State University of New York Press, 1995).

3. Kenneth Grahame, *The Wind in the Willows* (New York: Charles Scribner's Sons, 1933), 161–63.

Chapter 8. Wrestling with Wrath

1. This reading of the story is reinforced by Everett Fox's masterful translation of the text, which hugs close to the Hebrew word order and literal word meanings. It becomes clear that Cain hides himself from the Presence, rather than being banished from it: "my iniquity is too great to be borne . . . and from your face must I conceal myself" (Gen. 4:13-14). See Everett Fox, trans., *The Five Books of Moses: Genesis, Exodus, Leviticus, Numbers, Deuteronomy* (New York: Schocken Books, 1995), 27.

2. See references for *anger, to be angry,* and *wrath* in Robert Young, *Young's Analytical Concordance to the Bible* (Peabody, Mass.: Hendrickson Publishers), 38–39, 1076–77.

3. This is the way the ancient rabbis understand the struggle between wrath and mercy in the biblical tales. They know it is figurative language, not a literal glimpse into the workings of the divine Mystery. The Talmud goes so far as to imagine God lamenting the destruction of the Flood, "When I conquer, I

lose. . . . for I destroyed my world." See C. G. Montefiore and H. Loewe, comps., *A Rabbinic Anthology* (New York: Schocken Books, 1974), 40.

4. The wrath and mercy of God are, of course, themes from Genesis to Revelation, invoked in the sayings of Jesus and the teaching of Saint Paul, not just in the Old Testament.

5. I am indebted to my university professor Rabbi Judah Golden, first to hold the chair of Jewish Studies at Yale back in the 1960s, for this clear, textually rooted approach to the Genesis text. Note that the text tells us clearly: "The LORD said, 'Shall I hide from Abraham what I am about to do . . . ? No, for I have chosen him, that he may charge his children and his household after him to keep the way of the LORD by doing righteousness and justice'" (Gen. 18:17-19).

6. Thus God says, "I must go down and see. . . and if not, I will know," presuming innocence, rather than "and if the outcry is true, I will know," indicating the probability of guilt. The sins of the infamous cities, chiefly arrogant wealth and oppression of the poor, are described in Jeremiah 23:14 and Ezekiel 16:49 as well as Genesis 19. Put all together, these sins form the epitome in ancient legend of corrupt humanity—oppressing the poor; turning widows out to starve; readiness to rob, rape, or kill travelers stopping for the night, or daughters of minority groups, in violation of the ancient code of protection for the wayfarer.

Chapter 9. Ordinary Resurrections: Dealing with Depression

1. This and subsequent prayers are from my journal. The style is based on Holy Week and Easter hymns of the Eastern Church.

2. John 11:25, Greek text.

3. Rabbi Jules Harlow, ed., *Mahzor for Rosh Hashanah and Yom Kippur: A Prayer Book for the Days of Awe* (New York: Rabbinical Assembly, 1972), 61.

4. See Edwards, *Living Simply through the Day: Spiritual Survival in a Complex Age*, 148.

5. Torah interpretation derived from Rabbi Shefa Gold. Used by permission.

6. See 2 Timothy 1:9–10: "This grace . . . has now been revealed through the appearing of our Savior Christ Jesus, who abolished death and brought life and immortality to light through the gospel." Note that grace, life, and immortality are all connected with the whole "appearing" of Christ and with the good news itself. This entire chapter is based on the Christ the Victor motif in the writings of the church fathers, as revived by Gustav Aulen in his much-neglected classic *Christus Victor*, and as still taught in the Eastern Church.

7. John 1:3-4, my translation, based on the discussion in Raymond E. Brown, *The Gospel according to John (1–12)*, 2d ed., The Anchor Bible, vol. 29 (Garden City, N.Y.: Doubleday & Company, 1982): 6–7. The Greek can be translated many ways. Brown says this is a possible rendering but that the Evangelist couldn't possibly have meant it! The conventional tendency to divorce *zoe* from the everyday world bends translations to predetermined expectations.

8. New Testament writers are not shy about nature metaphors for Christ's resurrection power. Jesus himself is heard to say, "Unless a grain of wheat falls into the earth and dies, it remains just a single grain" in John 12:24; Saint Paul uses the seed metaphor for resurrection in 1 Corinthians 15:37, and it is common in the church fathers.

Chapter 10. Holy and Glorious Flesh: The Challenge of Sexual Enticement

1. I am using the tripartite biblical distinction of flesh, soul, and spirit to stand as real ways we experience the different levels of the whole person, without suggesting they are separate realities.

2. This fact is largely hidden from modern readers by the zeal of modern translators to make sure everything is easy for readers

to understand. Thus *heart* is translated "mind," *bowels* becomes "compassion," etc.

3. The very word for mercy or pity in Hebrew, *rachamim,* means "womb-feeling."

4. These reports have appeared in the Science pages of the *New York Times.* See especially Sandra Blakeslee, "Complex and Hidden Brain in Gut Makes Stomachaches and Butterflies," *New York Times,* 23 January, 1996, Science section; and Jacqueline Boone, review of *The Second Brain: The Scientific Basis of Gut Instinct and a Groundbreaking New Understanding of Nervous Disorders of the Stomach and Intestine,* by Michael D. Gershon, *New York Times,* 17 January, 1999, sec. 7, p. 21. For further reading, see Dean Ornish, M.D., *Love and Survival: The Scientific Basis for the Healing Power of Intimacy* (New York: HarperCollins Publishers, 1998). These discoveries also parallel the "energy" medicine of China and India, which, like Hebrew culture, experience "centers of energy" in the body and are the subject of medical investigation at Harvard Medical School and other places. For my own prayer exercises based on the research, write Interweave, P.O. Box 1516, Summit, NJ 07901; call 973-763-8312; or e-mail through Web site: www.interweave.org.

5. Harlow, ed., *Mahzor for Rosh Hashanah and Yom Kippur,* 59–61. This ancient prayer, probably dating to the time of Jesus, is used every morning.

6. See Carmichael, *Carmina Gadelica,* 199: prayer 226.

7. Williams's unique approach to the sanctification of eros is found in his *Outlines of Romantic Theology, with which is reprinted Religion and Love in Dante: The Theology of Romantic Love,* ed. Alice Mary Hadfield (Grand Rapids, Mich.: William B. Eerdmans Publishing Company, 1990), 9.

8. This gotta-have-it agony is what Scripture and tradition call *porneia*—lust, or concupiscence—a state of mental attitude more than a state of body. It parallels the Buddhist idea of "craving" as the source of our spiritual suffering.

9. Carmichael, *Carmina Gadelica,* 199, prayer 226.

10. This theological slogan of Saint Athanasius asserted that unless the Divine had, in Christ, taken a full and complete human soul and body into union with itself, human nature was incapable of full redemption, and only "souls" would be saved.

11. Williams, *Outlines of Romantic Theology*, 111.

12. Gregory of Nyssa, *The Life of Moses,* trans. Abraham J. Malherbe and Everett Ferguson (New York: Paulist Press, 1978), 110–11.

13. Thomas Mann, *Joseph and His Brothers,* trans. H.T. Lowe-Porter (New York: Alfred A. Knopf, 1974), 749.

14. See Michael Murphy, *The Future of the Body: Explorations into the Further Evolution of Human Nature* (Los Angeles: Jeremy P. Tarcher, 1992), 505–7.

15. From a 1965 conversation with Father William Austin, sometime Anglican missionary to Korea, now deceased.

Chapter 11. Busyness and Sabbath Time

1. *Prayer Book and Hymnal: Containing The Book of Common Prayer and The Hymnal 1982 according to the Use of The Episcopal Church* (New York: Church Hymnal Corporation, 1986), 820.

2. See Genesis 2:2-3.

3. There is a long history of variety and dispute about exactly how to celebrate the Lord's Day and the status of the seventh-day Sabbath for Christians. Early Jewish Christians kept both. For an illuminating history see Tilden Edwards, "The Sabbath in History," pt. 2 of *Sabbath Time*, rev. ed. (Nashville, Tenn.: Upper Room Books, 2003).

4. Jesus' disputes with other Jews are about details of Sabbath observance, not the substance of the Sabbath commandment. See Montefiore and Loewe, "The Commandments, the Sabbath, and the Law," chap. 7 in *A Rabbinic Anthology,* for a wealth of rabbinical quotes about the Sabbath.

5. My thanks to Rabbi William Horn of the Jewish Community Center in Summit, New Jersey, for double-checking my

Sabbath information. Today the full Sabbath observance described is found only in traditional Orthodox and Hasidic circles.

6. This symbol of the Presence is related to the figure of Holy Wisdom in Proverbs 8 and is the feminine manifestation of God in traditional Judaism, where she is imagined "in exile" with the people of God, a sustaining presence helping Israel prepare for Messiah's coming.

7. See Edwards, "Living a Sabbath Day," pt. 4 in *Sabbath Time.*

8. See Rodger Kamenetz, "Rabbi Shefa Gold: The Essential Vehicle," chap. 7 in *Stalking Elijah: Adventures with Today's Jewish Mystical Masters* (San Francisco: HarperSanFrancisco, 1997), for a description of Shefa's approach to liturgy.

Chapter 13. Christ and Caesar: Taming the Pecking Order

1. I am indebted for this description of Roman society to the well-researched Masters of Rome Series of Colleen McCullough, which trace the rise of the "Great Man" to prominence in Rome from 100 B.C. through the life of Julius Caesar. See *The First Man in Rome, The Grass Crown, Fortune's Favorites, Caesar's Women, Caesar: Let the Dice Fly.* Published by William Morrow and Company.

2. "Holy Baptism" in *The Book of Common Prayer* (New York: Church Pension Fund, 1945), 277.

3. For an in-depth overview of the organization of Roman cities, see Wayne A. Meeks, *The First Urban Christians: The Social World of the Apostle Paul* (New Haven, Conn.: Yale University Press, 1983).

4. "These are the things, the fruits of which a man enjoys in this world, while the stock remains for him for the world to come: viz., honoring father and mother, the practice of charity." A. Th. Philips, "Morning Service," in *Daily Prayers with English Translation,* rev. ed. (New York: Hebrew Publishing Company, n.d.), 19, 21. Also see Harlow, *Mahzor for Rosh Hashanah and Yom Kippur,* 67.

5. I am indebted to Donald Hoad of Calvary Church, Summit, New Jersey, for this valuable interpretation of Jesus' saying.

6. See Deikman, "Mental Health, Aging, and the Role of Service," 5.

Chapter 14. Facing Evil: The Temptation of Malign Will

1. For a remarkable modern reinterpretation of the New Testament's vision of "principalities and powers," combining depth psychology and liberation theology, see Walter Wink's Powers Series: *Naming the Powers: The Language of Power in the New Testament* (1984), *Unmasking the Powers: The Invisible Forces That Determine Human Existence* (1986), *Engaging the Powers: Discernment and Resistance in a World of Domination* (1992). Published by Fortress Press, Minneapolis, Minn.

2. Charles Williams, *War in Heaven* (Grand Rapids, Mich.: William B. Eerdmans Publishing Company, 1970), 244–45.

3. "Holy Eucharistic I" in *Prayer Book and Hymnal,* 334.

4. Eugene Peterson, *Answering God: The Psalms As Tools for Prayer* (San Francisco: HarperSanFrancisco, 1989), 122.

Part Three: Offering the Self for Partnership

1. The entity God shapes out of the "dust of the ground," *adamah,* is called *ha-adam,* literally, "the earthling." (Adam, here, is not a proper name.) This creature is not called man, *iysh,* or woman, *ishshah,* until the separation of one part of the earthperson from another.

2. These primal tasks of humanity are derived from the creation narratives in Genesis 1–2.

Chapter 15. Befriending the Soul in Self and Others

1. I am indebted to Sister Ellen Stephen of the Order of Saint Helena for this piece of Bernard's teaching. See Doug Shadel

and Ellen Stephen, *Vessel of Peace: The Voyage towards Spiritual Freedom* (Scattle, Wash.: Three Tree Press, 2000), 185. It is quite true that Saint Bernard would not have as positive a view of "healthy narcissism" as I am asserting. Modern psychology has revealed dynamics of the soul not sufficiently appreciated by the ancients. For a clear discussion of a Christian perspective on self-acceptance rooted in post-Freudian thought, see M. Scott Peck, M.D., *The Road Less Traveled: A New Psychology of Love, Traditional Values and Spiritual Growth* (New York: Simon and Schuster, 1978), chapter 1.

2. See James Russell Lowell, "Once to Ev'ry Man and Nation" in *The Hymnal 1940* (New York: Church Pension Fund, 1943), hymn 519.

3. Charles Williams, *The Greater Trumps* (Grand Rapids, Mich.: William B. Eerdmans Publishing Company, 1976), 136.

4. See especially "The Social Dimension in Prayer: Intercession" in Douglas V. Steere, *Dimensions of Prayer: Cultivating a Relationship with God,* rev. ed. (Nashville, Tenn.: Upper Room Books, 1997), 66–68.

Chapter 16. Learning to Pray with the World Again: Invoking the Creatures

1. Ewert Cousins, trans., "The Life of Saint Francis," in *Bonaventure* (New York: Paulist Press, 1978), 258. Bonaventure's work collects many eyewitness accounts of the saint's life.

2. Ibid., 254–55.

3. See, for example, *Prayer Book and Hymnal,* 47–49.

4. Saint Patrick's *Lorica* or Breastplate, trans. by Cecil Frances Alexander, "The Holy Trinity," in *The Hymnal 1982: According to the Use of The Episcopal Church* (New York: Church Hymnal Corporation, 1985), hymn 370.

5. Cousins, in *Bonaventure,* 257–58.

6. Henry Beston, *The Outermost House: A Year of Life on the Great Beach of Cape Cod* (New York: Henry Holt and Company, 1992), 25.

Chapter 17. The Art of Unceasing Prayer: Growing Up into God's Life

1. The rich variety of Hebrew words includes *bea,* "to petition"; *athar,* "to entreat"; *paga,* "to intercede or strike against"; *palal,* "to judge self"; *tsela,* "to bow or bend"; *siyach,* "to meditate"; *shaal,* "to ask"; *chalah,* "to smooth down or deprecate"; *tephillah,* "a prayer of praise"; *lachash,* "a whisper." In Greek, *deomai,* "to want"; *erotao,* "to interrogate"; *euchomai,* "to wish"; *parakaleo,* "to call beside someone, or advocate"; *proseuche,* "pray earnestly; a pouring out."

2. James Montgomery, "Prayer Is the Soul's Sincere Desire," *The Hymnal of the Protestant Episcopal Church in the United States of America 1940* (New York: Church Pension Fund, 1961), hymn 419.

3. I do not mean to denigrate contemplation as a form of prayer, just the notion that desire itself is undesirable. Christian spirituality was deeply influenced by Stoic philosophy, which emphasized *apatheia,* "the stilling of all passions." Sometimes this was misunderstood to include the complete eradication of natural desire, rather than its progressive freedom from distortions and attachments.

4. The Greek text of Luke 11:9 uses present progressives for "ask, seek, find," indicating ongoing activity.

ABOUT THE AUTHOR

Robert Corin Morris is an Episcopal priest in full-time teaching ministry as executive director of Interweave, Inc., a community learning center in Summit, New Jersey. Morris founded Interweave in 1980 to help people change their daily habits in ways that foster wellness, deepen spirituality, and promote the common good in families and communities. As director and lead teacher, he teaches, offers spiritual direction, and speaks in parishes, at conferences, and at retreats. The author has been active in Jewish-Christian and Buddhist-Christian dialogue.

Morris received his undergraduate degree from Yale University and his Bachelor of Sacred Theology from The General Theological Seminary. In addition, he has received training in mind-body medicine meditation methods and earned his certificate in spiritual direction from the Shalem Institute for Spiritual Formation.

Further information about Interweave is available at www.interweave.org and by e-mail, information@interweave.org.

OTHER TITLES OF INTEREST
from Upper Room Books

A Book of Personal Prayer
compiled by René Bideaux
0-8358-0812-2

Discovering Community:
A Meditation on Community in Christ
by Stephen V. Doughty
0-8358-0870-X

Finding a Spiritual Friend: How Friends and
Mentors Can Make Your Faith Grow
by Timothy Jones
0-8358-0857-2

Forgiveness, the Passionate Journey:
Nine Steps of Forgiving through Jesus' Beatitudes
by Flora Slosson Wuellner
0-8358-0945-5

Heart Whispers: Benedictine Wisdom for Today
by Elizabeth Canham
0-8358-0892-0

Release:
Healing from Wounds of Family, Church,
and Community
by Flora Slosson Wuellner
0-8358-0775-4

These titles are available from Upper Room Books online
www.upperroom.org/bookstore

by telephone
1-800-972-0433

or through your local bookstore.